MAKING
PAPER
TOYS

Also by Carson I. A. Ritchie
Bone and Horn Carving: A Pictorial History
Carving Shells and Cameos
The Eskimo and His Art
Making Scientific Toys
Organic Jewellery You Can Make
Shell Carving: History and Techniques
Soft Stone Carving

MAKING PAPER TOYS *by Carson I. A. Ritchie*

LUTTERWORTH PRESS
GUILDFORD AND LONDON

First published 1978

ISBN 0 7188 2352 4

Copyright © 1978, Carson I. A. Ritchie

All Rights Reserved. No part of this publication may be reproduced, stored in a retrieval system, or transmitted, in any form or by any means, electronic, mechanical, photocopying, recording or otherwise, without the prior permission of Lutterworth Press, Farnham Road, Guildford, Surrey.

Photoset, printed and bound
in Great Britain by
REDWOOD BURN LIMITED
Trowbridge & Esher

CONTENTS

INTRODUCTION   7

1. MATERIALS AND TOOLS   10
   Varieties of Paper for Use, 10, Useful Tools,
   16, Adhesives, 17

2. THE PAPER DOLL AND MAGNETIC PLANNING TAPE
   TOYS   20
   Paper Doll and Accessories, 20, Chinese
   General, 28, Magnetic Chess and Draughts,
   30, Air Circus, 32, Deep Diving Game, 36,
   Air Battle Games, 36, Climbing Game, 38

3. PAPIER MÂCHÉ TOYS   40
   Basic Mixture, 42, Sculptured Toys, 43,
   Daruma or Japanese Tumbler, 44, Ninepins,
   47

4. WAR GAMING IN PAPER   49
   Making the Models, 51, Mounting the
   Pieces, 53, Cutting out the Pieces, 56, Battlefield
   Accessories, 62, A War Game from
   Ancient China, 63

5. TOYS MADE FROM MIRROR PAPER   66
   Heliograph, 67, Designoscope, 71, Kaleidoscope,
   75, Periscope, 79, Polyoptic Mirrors,
   81, Distorting Mirrors, 82,
   Praxinoscope, 83

Contents

6. **PAPER ENTERTAINMENTS** — 88
   Diorama, 88, The Peepshow and Pepper's Ghost, 97, Panorama, 102

7. **TOY THEATRES** — 106
   Constructing a Theatre, 109, The Shadow Theatre, 117

8. **HOT AIR BALLOONS AND SPINNERS** — 119
   Hot Air Balloon, 119, The Spinner, 123

9. **MISCELLANEOUS TOYS** — 125
   Jigsaw Puzzle, 125, The Pantin, 129, Thaumatrope, 132, Rotater, 133, Paper Barometer, 135, Weather House, 136, Paper Flower, 136, Party Puzzles, 137

INDEX — 140

Introduction

I can still remember the enjoyment I got as a child from making up my own paper toys and playing with them. Other people have discovered the amusement value of paper toys. Hans Christian Andersen used to make paper cuts to amuse children — a paper toy of his is used as an illustration in this book. Curiously enough, another very famous story teller for children, Lewis Carroll, also used to make paper playthings to amuse children — he even carried a box of them on train journeys so that he could amuse any small fellow travellers who were becoming bored with the journey.

Ever since its invention by the Chinese paper has been used for toys, but nowadays there are more kinds of paper than there have ever been before. I have tried to keep up with the new kinds of paper that have been invented by describing toys that can be made from them. All the toys in this book are either well-tried traditional ones, or toys I have invented myself. Some of the old toys may suggest all sorts of ideas to my readers. If they make a model paper balloon, they might want to read a little about the history of hot-air balloons in this country, or in America. If they make a heliograph they might even start looking at history books to find out when heliographs were really used to keep scouting columns of armies in touch with the main body when they were operating in enemy territory. This happened in many of the Colonial Wars in the nineteenth century, particularly in Southern Africa.

Figure 1. An example of an intricate papercut by Hans Christian Andersen.

Paper offers many advantages as a material for toys. There is nothing poisonous about paper, so children can handle it safely. It is a lot cheaper than many other toy materials. Sometimes, when other materials such as wood, become expensive, people start working in paper. This happened after the Second World War, when Polish sculptors began to work in paper because that was all they could afford. Other sculptors in different countries followed suit, so did window designers, and paper sculpture became a big craze. Some of the toys in this book can be made by recycling paper, and everyone seems to be agreed nowadays that re-cycling is a good idea. Any pieces of paper that are left over from making the toys can also be cut up and used again as *papier mâché*, so there is nothing wasted.

It does not require any great effort to make paper toys and even small children, or the handicapped, could make at least some of the toys described in this book. Small children can be

Introduction

given safety scissors, so that they can cut the paper without the risk of harming themselves.

Paper is a very stimulating material to work with. You can make something out of it, and then, if it is a success, make the object again in some other, more durable material. If for example you enjoyed making the periscope in mirror paper, you might decide to make another one, this time with real mirrors (see my companion volume to this book, *Making Scientific Toys*, Lutterworth, 1978).

1. Materials and Tools

The Varieties of Paper for Use
There are two ways of making paper: by hand or by machine. Handmade paper is made by a craftsman who dips a frame or "mould" into a vat of vegetable pulp made up from the unbroken fibres of linen rag, special grass, bark or, in the case of Eastern paper-making, bamboo. Machine-made paper is made from pulp which is drawn from a vat and rolled between rollers. The difference between handmade paper and machine-made papers usually shows up at a glance. Often handmade paper is thicker and heavier. It usually shows the lines of the frame or mould when held up to the light, and often there is a distinctive watermark. Differences between machine-made papers usually have to do with the material from which they are made (various ingredients such as china clay may be added as binding agents) and the way in which they are finished. Often a paper will have a glossy appearance because it has been "hot pressed" between rollers and sometimes polished as well.

Whether made in China and Japan or Europe, handmade papers are invariably more expensive than machine-made papers and there are only a few types available. Machine-made papers are very suitable for basic toymaking. Handmade papers, especially the patterned ones, are very useful for the decorations to put on the outside of a toy. Thus a paper doll might be made from ordinary paper but the dresses could be made from a colour-patterned Japanese paper.

Unlike handmade papers from Japan, Britain, or America, of which only a few types are produced, there is an enormous choice of machine-made papers. What is more, machine-made paper is very cheap compared with the handmade variety.

Materials and Tools

The reason that papers differ in appearance is due not merely to the material from which they are made but to the finishing process they go through. Paper may be dampened to bring the minerals in it to the surface, thus giving it a glazed finish. It may be polished to a smooth surface between cylinders, or given a very high gloss indeed. Machine-made paper is weaker in the direction in which the rollers on the machine were moving and stronger at right angles to them. The direction of strength can be determined by simply tearing the paper. Of course it is often useful to apply this test and to use the paper so that it is folded correctly to have maximum strength.

A paper's strength is also determined by its raw material. Newspaper is made from wood pulp and some pulps are stronger than others. Soda pulp paper, made from deciduous trees is weaker than sulphite pulp, made from pine and spruce. This in turn is weaker than sulphate pulp paper, the familiar "kraft" paper used for brown wrapping paper, which is made from strong coniferous trees.

As a toy's life depends on its strength it is obviously good policy to look out for strong papers for its foundation, even though it may have a top covering of thin fancy paper. Roughly speaking, the darker a paper is the stronger it is. Esparto grass paper, used for writing paper and stamps, is light, clear, and has little strength. Manilla grass, the dark fibre that gives us "Manilla" envelopes is dark and sometimes so strong as to be virtually untearable.

Another very obvious way of strengthening paper is to double it with more paper. Paper so treated may be turned either into a "fancy" paper with a decorative surface, or a "board". As many of the toys described in this book are made partly from board, and as the book itself is about paper toys, it is perhaps worth emphasizing that board itself is constructed from paper. Board, or "cardboard" as it is more usually called, is often a sandwich of different papers, glued and pressed together. A good example of board is the mounting board used as a "mat" or an interior frame for pictures. This mounting board is made up in Japan of high-grade paper, pressed on to the top of a pulped inner sheet, the other side of the "sandwich" being a sheet of plain white paper. Mounting board is a simple three-fold sandwich. Other boards are more elaborate. Some of them have six, or even eight "webs" or layers of paper pressed together to make one thickness of board.

The reader should find out for himself the kinship between board and paper by making up his own boards from thicknesses of paper wound round one another and stuck together. These home-made boards will prove especially useful for odd shapes — such as the cardboard cylinder used for the heliograph. It is worthwhile making other boards, flat ones, which can be given decorative treatment. Even the humblest board, made from sheets of old waste paper that have been pasted and pressed together, will come to life when surfaced with a patchwork quilt design of scraps of differently coloured tissue paper.

The paper worker should be prepared to adapt anything he has to meet his special needs. A great deal of paper can be had free. He or she must become a tireless collector of this scrap, keeping anything that would appear to be useful, pressed flat under a heavy weight, between two sheets of *backing board* (heavy cardboard which can be bought from art suppliers and which has a multitude of uses). *Kraft paper* and *manilla paper* have already been mentioned. They can be obtained for nothing in the shape of parcel paper and envelopes. *Cartridge paper*, a thin card similar to *Bristol board*, provides most of the box packaging for the confectionery trade. *Waxed paper*, so difficult to buy from paper stockists, can be obtained free in the shape of the lining of boxes of breakfast cereals. *Tissue paper*, which is also used to wrap many purchases, is very useful. Like other papers it can be stained to the desired colour, from white, with packets of Revlon dyes or other fabric dyes. *Newsprint* is the rough, absorbent paper on which all newspapers are printed, except for air mail editions and a special edition of the *Times*, which is printed on rag paper for a few important people, such as the Queen and the Archbishop of Canterbury. *Board* can be obtained for the trouble of picking up and carrying away empty boxes in any supermarket. Though the board in these boxes might at first sight appear too thin to be useful, its usefulness can be increased by pasting it and pressing it to other board of the same thickness. If PVA adhesive is used for this purpose a very hard board indeed can be obtained. This home-made board rivals, but does not equal in strength the *millboard* or *strawboard*, which was used before the First World War for making covers for books. Never

Materials and Tools

refuse the gift of an old book, however unreadable it may be. Its covers, torn off and stripped of their cloth covering, make ideal board, even after years of use.

We now leave papers that can be obtained free and come to bought papers. There is no one shop to which a paper craftsman should go. Instead he should try to vary his suppliers as much as possible, persuading his local stockist to stock the papers he needs most, buying paper or cardboard from the mill if need be, and always remembering that the more you buy of anything the cheaper it will be. Paper is most expensive when sold by the sheet. Paint and wallpaper merchants often have bargains for the paper toy maker. My local paint shop stocks two grades of *shelf-lining paper*, one superior to the other. Both cost only a few pence for a roll containing many yards. This paper can be put to all kinds of uses. The same kind of shop often stocks *doll's house wallpaper*. This is manufactured in patterns which simulate squared stone walls, rough stone walling, brick, tile, slate, wood and even parquet flooring, as well as, of course, doll's house wallpaper. These specialist papers can also be obtained from a paper shop.

Printers and bookbinders consume large quantities of paper and board of many different kinds and thicknesses, all of which have to be cut to size for the job. Pieces cut off the shaped size in printing or binding are called *offcuts*. These cuttings can be purchased for a few pence. They may be just the size you want. Almost all the toys in this book were made from offcuts obtained from a professional sign printer. I got such large bundles of paper from this man that it was often difficult to carry them away.

The local art supplies shop offers a rich harvest. It usually stocks *Bristol board*, a thin card poster paper usually stocked in 20 × 30in. sizes,[1] *cartridge paper* usually sold in 20 × 30in.

[1] Now that Britain is going metric, papers are calculated according to the weight of a square metre per gram, while American papers are still reckoned in pounds. Good quality typing paper, "Bond", may weigh 71 grams, and thinner typing paper, "Bank", 45 grams. Formerly paper in Britain was calculated by its weight per *ream*. The word "ream" is a confusing one. Attempts have been made to standardize the British ream around 500 sheets, but it varies around this number according to the type of paper sold. The ream is divided into *quires*. A standard quire is one twentieth of a standard ream, that is 25 sheets. Once again the quire is a unit of measurement that can denote different amounts. Always ask how much you are getting in the ream or quire to avoid subsequent disappointment.

sheets, *crêpe paper*, sold in folded sheets, *tissue paper*, sold in folded sheets, quires, or packets containing sheets of different colours. Exotic tissue papers, such as *tie-dyed tissue*, have to be obtained from a specialist paper shop, unless, that is, you tie-dye them yourself, starting with white tissue. Dyeing paper is essential for getting just the shade you want. Mrs. Delany, the greatest of all British paper artists, spent a lot of thought and trouble getting the shade she wanted for her paper mosaic pictures.[2] In her time, the eighteenth century, you had to mix your own dyes. Now you can obtain them from any craft shop, in every conceivable shade, in conveniently small-sized packets. The packets contain instructions for dyeing, including how to tie-dye.[3]

An art supplier will certainly stock *newsprint*, just the same material on which your daily newspaper is printed. This paper is usually stocked in 20 × 30 in. sizes. Other papers which can be bought at this kind of shop include *play paper*, a lighter version of cartridge paper, which is obtainable by the sheet in many colours, *coloured art paper*, of similar weight, *detail paper*, a thin, cheap paper sold by the roll, *layout paper*, another thin paper which has many uses, *imitation parchment*, a thin, white, semi-translucent paper which, like *tracing paper*, is useful for making screens for shadow puppets.

The specialist paper shop (they exist in some large towns) fills in all the gaps in the paper range. You should be able to get any kind of paper from a shop of this sort. At the specialist paper shop you will certainly be tempted to buy some of the handmade *Japanese papers*, coloured or white, embossed or plain, that I referred to earlier. You will also see superior papers made in England, such as *Bockingford mould-made*; Cockerell and Swedish *marbled papers* will also be on show. You can hand-marble papers such as these for yourself, but it is a finicky process and requires special equipment. On the other hand, hand-marbled papers are very expensive indeed, whether they are made in England, Sweden or Italy. There is only one kind of paper that

---

[2] Carson I. A. Ritchie: *Art in Paper*, A. S. Barnes, New Jersey, U.S.A. and *Papercraft* in the "Teach Yourself" series, Hodder, England.

[3] Tie dying is a simple process by which part of a sheet of tissue or other thin paper is tied in a knot and dipped in dye. The knotted part is rejected by the dye. Fabric dyes can be used for dyeing paper and usually proprietary dyes give illustrations showing the kind of knots that can be tied.

Materials and Tools 15

you will pay more for, by the sheet, and that is Japanese paper. Swedish *Batik paper* is dyed in different colours by a special process. A great variety of art papers are available. They include: *art drawing paper, ticket lettering paper, My Tints, Ingres paper* (which can be obtained in various colours and which is sold in 19 × 25 in. sheets), *sugar paper* (a thin cartridge paper sold in 20 × 25 in. sheets), *Kent* (smooth drawing paper) and many more. *Blotting paper* is available in various colours. This is used in one of the toys I describe later and you may find other uses for it yourself. *Cover paper*, a stiffish, opaque paper sold in 20 × 30 in. sheets, is obtainable in many colours. *Matt surface paper* (a paper with different colours on each side) is also sold in 20 × 30 in. sheets.

Like the art suppliers, the specialist paper shop should also provide a good selection of boards of various weights. These include *very board*, sold in 20 × 25 in. sheets, *bending board, Super Exelda Ivory board*, matt or smooth, in 20 × 25 in. sheets, and a number of others.

Many customers probably enter a specialist paper shop to buy something quite ordinary, and come out having bought something rather exotic instead. Exotic papers on sale there include *Indian Fleck Unsized paper, Flint paper* with a smooth polished surface in 20 × 30 in. sheets of many colours, *Flower paper* in blue and pink, which has small whole dried flowers, which retain their original colour, stuck to the surface, *Chromo Lux*, a stiffish paper in many colours and several finishes such as gold, silver and copper which comes in 19 × 27 in. sheets, the thin, shiny-surfaced paper called *Glassline* and *Fleckpaper*, which has shiny fragments worked into its surface, *metallic foil papers*, including self-adhesive foils, patterned foils and crêped foils, *metallic foil boards, fluorescent paper* (ideal for making a spooky model haunted house) and *Cinemoid*, a translucent plastic sheet only available in colours.

Mirror papers are the kind of specialist papers which have many uses for toys, but about which the average reader might well have heard nothing. They are available in *Mellinex*, a mirror paper roll mirrored on both sides (which always seems a waste to me), self-adhesive *Silver Polyester* and *Silver* and *Coloured Mirriboard*, which are mirror papers in board form. Mirror paper will be used for the kaleidoscope and designoscope mentioned later, as well as for a number of other toys in this book.

How are the rather numerous kinds of paper I have mentioned essential for the toys in this book? Some materials I shall mention again and again, such as the *patterned papers*, the fancy wrapping papers which are used to wrap a completed toy and give it a gay exterior. Other kinds of materials will be mentioned rarely, and some not at all. It is worthwhile, however, to know just how extensive is the range of papers available. Often an exotic paper will suggest a toy. For example, why not make a paper doll of brightly patterned fabric papers and attach it with MPT in the way I shall describe later to a mount of Flower paper? The Flower paper mount could be trimmed with pressed gilt paper shells – just one of the many paper accessories which I have not had time to mention – and the whole concept would represent "Mary, Mary, Quite Contrary" in her garden. If you cannot get gilt paper shells, improvise. Buy small real shells from Friedleins, Natural Products, 718 Old Forest Road, London, E.3., gild them with *Goldfinger* and attach them with *PVA adhesive*.

Useful Tools

The mention of these two products brings me to the tools and materials required for paper working. These are neither very numerous, nor expensive, but it is handy to have them. Often the possession of a particular tool means all the difference between doing a very good job and doing a poor one. A *bookbinder's knife* is a useful acquisition. *Craft knives* of several different sizes are in some ways even more useful as they do not need to be sharpened. Have at least two craft knives, such as a *Stanley Kraft* knife and an *Xacto knife*. If you buy a bookbinder's knife, get a sharpening stone and some oil to sharpen it. To make sure that you are cutting board, or paper, straight, it is essential to have a *Straight Edge*. This is a tool that looks like a ruler but it is either all of metal, or it has a metal edge against which the knife edge is pressed while it is cutting. It is essential to try to cut *along* the straight edge, not *into* it, otherwise you will ruin the edge of your knife.

Always lay board, card, or anything that has to be cut, on a *cutting block*. It saves cutting into your working surface, such as the table or bench on which you work, it also saves dulling the edge of your knife. Soft wood does well, unless you let the grain

Materials and Tools

catch the point of the knife and draw it out of true. Cardboard is ideal, but it needs constant renewal and soon becomes too cut and hacked to give a flat surface. Hardboard lasts very well, but its hardness probably entails a lot of extra knife sharpening.

There is a specialist cutting tool for every job. If you have to cut a round hole, then use an *Xacto punch*. Use the smaller Xacto craft knives or a *stencil cutting knife* for cutting fine detail. Never, under any circumstances, use a razor blade, either shielded or unshielded. It is impossible to get the right balance. A craft knife, on the other hand, sits naturally in the fingers, like a pen.

Have several pairs of *scissors*. A large pair, with blades six inches or more long is very handy for roughing out. For elaborate paper cutting, in thin paper, there is nothing like a pair of good *embroidery scissors* with blades about one and a quarter inches long. Keep them, carefully shielded from contact with any other objects, in the plastic wallet in which you bought them.

Other tools should include a long and a short *ruler*, a small clear plastic ruler, a clear plastic *set square* and a *circle protractor*. Though not essential at the outset, continued paper toy making will reveal the value of *French curves* and other templates for various shapes, such as are sold to draughtsmen.

Mention of draughtsmen recalls their special tool, the pen. A *Rapidograph pen* will prove very useful; a *compass* and *dividers* are also useful.

Adhesives

To function properly, a toy must be well put together. A good stock of adhesives and pastes helps towards this end. If you have to stick a small quantity of some material to paper, such as a square of MPT, use *Uhu glue*. *Aerosol adhesives* include *Scotch Photo mount* and *Scotch Spray mount*. These are very useful, but also very expensive. *Mounting tissue* is very much cheaper. It is tissue paper, coated on both sides with shellac. Give one edge of it a dab with a very hot smoothing iron and lay it on a mounting sheet. This will position it, and make sure it stays in place. Now lay the sheet with the mounting tissue attached to it, facing downwards, on top of the board that is to be the permanent mount. Lay a sheet of waste paper on top of the sandwich of print-mounting tissue – and board – and iron on top of it with a hot iron.

Cow gum is a thick, hard-holding adhesive. So too is *Copydex*, a petroleum-based adhesive made from rubber, which dries almost instantly and sets with a very hard join. The last two adhesives which I mentioned are insoluble in water. So too is *Gloy Studio gum*. This is a rubber solution in a petroleum mixture. The gum is spread thinly on one surface only and the work to be pasted can then be lifted, peeled off the sheet to which it is meant to adhere, and repositioned if need be. Studio gum is useful, but it has a tendency to sink into thin and absorbent paper and show up on the outside. So use Studio gum with thicker papers only. Lighter fuel will clean brushes clogged with Studio gum.

Pritt Cream adhesive, and *Pritt Non-Stringing Clear adhesive* are very popular with paperworkers. They come in handy sized containers. There is also *Pritt Dab-On tube*. No stick adhesive can, I feel, be completely non-sticky. Sooner or later some adhesive is bound to adhere to the hands, and then to some unwanted part of the work. You can, however, stave off this moment by wrapping the stick in a paper handkerchief and changing it for a new one the moment it becomes sticky.

PVA adhesive is mentioned more times in this book than any other kind. This is because of its successful use over the years by bookbinders. It is so strong that it binds the pages of the London Telephone Directory together, just by being brushed on to the back of the loose leaves. You can pick up the whole directory by one leaf and it will not let go. PVA really welds two pieces of cardboard together. If they are clipped in position and well brushed with the adhesive they will unite. What is more, brushing over card with PVA strengthens the card.

Sellotape is an invaluable asset for paper fastening, and *double-sided sellotape* provides the answer to the problem of fastening down Mellinex (mirror paper). Some adhesives can destroy the mirror-like quality of Mellinex but it can be safely sellotaped, stapled, or stuck down with a special builder's adhesive called *Dunlop Thixofix*. This thick adhesive, which is sold with a special spreader and which can be bought in most DIY (Do-it-Yourself) shops, allows two sheets to be pushed together until they have reached the right position before a bond is made.

The cheapest adhesive is one that you can make for yourself, and it is probably one of the most useful. It is cold water paste,

Materials and Tools

and is made with flour (preferably the plain, not the self-raising variety). Make up the paste by putting a tablespoonful of flour into a teacup, adding enough water to it to allow it to be stirred into a stiff cream, then topping it up with boiling water. At this point the whole mixture is tipped into a saucepan, and boiled gently for a few minutes. The mixture is now well stirred with a wooden spoon while boiling. Home-made paste of this sort does not keep for very long before it goes mouldy, but you can lengthen its life by adding a little alum (half a teaspoonful) to the mixture while it is cooling and by keeping it, not in a bowl, but in a screw top jar. Do not mix up more of the paste than you need at one time. The strength of cold water paste is such that the document repairers at the Public Record Office in London used, as a demonstration, to paste one side of a pound note to a sheet of bank paper and the other to a second sheet. The sheets were then pulled apart, thus splitting the note in two.

Every toy should look bright and cheerful when it is finished. A good finish can be assured by covering it in one of the fancy papers that has been mentioned or by painting it with *gouache* and *poster paint*. These paints give bright, solid colours to the small surfaces of the toys. Other colouring materials include: *Letrafilm*, a sheet of transparent coloured plastic that can be stuck down directly on to a black and white original. *Transeal* is another product of the same type.

All paints that are marketed in aerosol bottles or tins in England will have to be exchanged for liquid paint blown on with an airbrush in America. Lastly, a set of good *artist's water colours*, with brushes will prove useful for many jobs. For the special toy, such as a military miniature, *gold and silver leaf* are available in books. They are applied by being dabbed on over *artist's size*.

2. The Paper Doll and Magnetic Planning Tape Toys

Paper Dolls

There is no toy that recalls the childhood of mankind more than the paper doll. Even now, paper dolls act as substitutes for the spirits of Japanese children during the Shinto ceremonies. In Mexico dolls are made from *amatyl* paper, which also have a magical significance. Like the Japanese Shinto doll, these dolls are often just a sheet of paper cut into an outline and folded. Sometimes they are cut from many coloured layers of tissue paper sewn together. It is perfectly easy to make these dolls using a craft knife or a pair of embroidery scissors and they form a useful kind of 'instant' toy, like the paper patterns Hans Anderson used to cut out to amuse children.

Yet when I hear the words "paper doll" I think, not of Mexico or Japan, but of the paper dolls of my childhood. These were

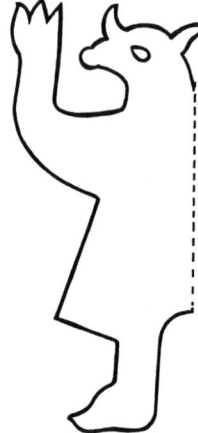

Figure 2. Amatyl paper doll, Mexico.

Figure 3. Enid, with complete Costermonger outfit.

figures printed in magazines or newspapers, which were still being published in the middle thirties. They were a series of prints showing a figure and an accompanying wardrobe for dressing it. Doll and wardrobe were cut out of the paper and then the clothes were hung on the doll by means of small tabs attached to the various items of dress, which slotted into slits cut in the doll's outline. Though they were by then experiencing a more limited existence, paper dolls had enjoyed a very long history. They had been invented in England in 1790, or thereabouts, and many of them were exported to France where they were called "English Dolls". The paper doll was a delightful invention with only one drawback. The tabs were tricky to cut out, and either they tore when folded over or shortly afterwards broke away once they began to take the strain of being handled in order to change the doll's clothes. These drawbacks did not deter the paper doll fancier of those days. Dolls of this sort cost nothing, because newspapers and magazines, as well as the suppliers of breakfast foods, often provided them for their customers. One of the joys of the paper doll was that it never lasted so long that it became a bore. Another was that it was only in paper that dolls were able to have anything like a complete wardrobe, all other materials being too expensive.

In this chapter, I have designed for readers a doll which requires no slots or tabs. All the clothes on this doll — whom, for convenience, we will call Enid — hang on her because her body has inset in it small sections of Magnetic Planning Tape (or MPT for short), and other pieces of tape are pasted to the underside of her clothes. There is consequently no wear and tear about dressing and undressing Enid. Her wardrobe, and the doll herself, ought in consequence to last a lot longer.

Figure 4. Front and back views of Enid and position of Magnetic Planning Tape on basic outline figure.

Front view

The Paper Doll

MPT is a plastic ribbon filled with magnetized iron oxide, the same substance that appears in tape recording tapes. It is used for constructing diagrams, such as sales charts, on a specially magnetized blackboard. It is not necessary to buy this blackboard, which is just as well owing to its expense. Instead, pieces of MPT will be placed in suitable spots on the backing board of all the toys that I am going to describe in this chapter. Another piece of MPT, this time attached to another part of the toy, will be placed on them and make magnetic contact, constituting as it were a magnetic nail holding the two parts of the toy in place. A square centimetre of MPT will support about 400 square centimetres of typing paper, depending on the weight of the paper. It

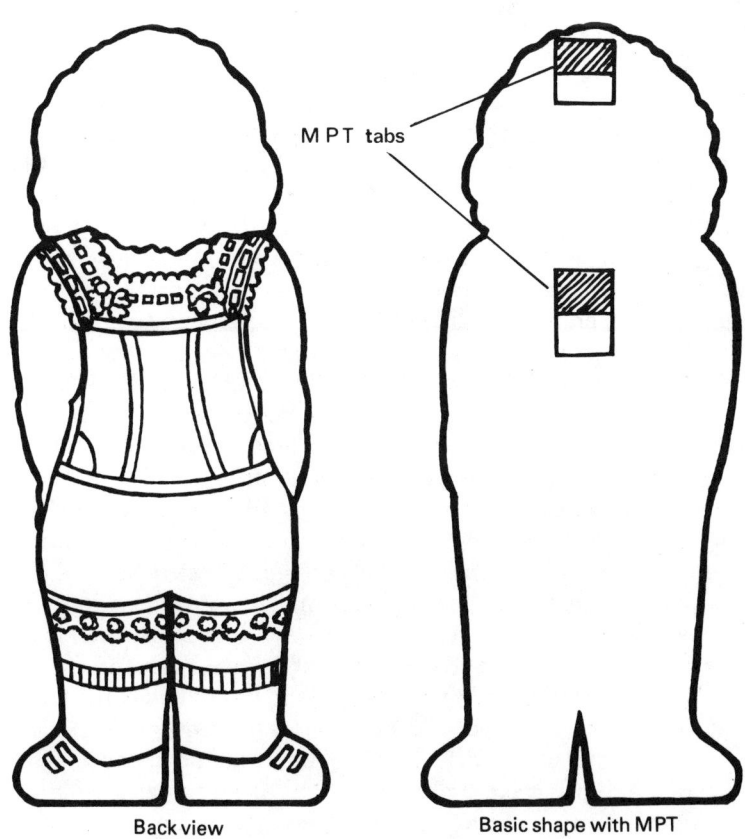

Back view   Basic shape with MPT

always pays to use more rather than less MPT so as to ensure a good contact. MPT is not expensive, it works out at about 2p. an inch. It is sold in two principal widths, 5 millimetres (3/16 in.) in a roll of two metres (78 in.) and 10 millimetres (3/8 in.) sold in rolls of one metre (39 in.). The references for the two sizes are "MT5" and "MT10".

The technique of applying MPT is very simple. The black side of the tape (containing magnetized iron particles) sticks to the black side of any other piece of tape — white will not stick to black. If you have a two-sided doll — like Enid — she must have pieces of tape facing both ways pasted between the printed sheets that constitute the front and back of the figure.

To assemble Enid, xerox the front and back view of her, along with her clothes. Now get a piece of card about the same thickness as the MPT, that is roughly one millimetre. Trace Enid's silhouette on to the card. It is the same front and back. As we are working with a rather small figure, the MPT attachments are going to be smaller than would otherwise have been wished. Cut two square holes in the figure to hold the MPT insets that are going to keep Enid's clothes in place. Use a sharp craft knife and a straight edge to do this. Cut a hole 1 cm (2/5 in.) square just below the hair line, and another the same size in the chest. Now cut round Enid's silhouette in the card with a stencil cutter or small sharp craft knife. Cut out Enid's back view and paste it on to the back of the card outline. Use embroidery scissors to cut round the outline in the xerox paper. Paste this paper back view on to one side of the card silhouette, using PVA, and rubbing down well with a bone folder so as to prevent wrinkling. When dry, take 2 cm (3/4 in.) lengths of the *smaller* size of MPT (a $\frac{1}{2}$ cm wide) and paste them into the recess so that you have a white slip and a black slip laid on top of one another. These slips face different ways so that they can hold on Enid's back headdress or hat, and her front headgear at the same time. Position similarly cut strips in the chest, laid the same way. Now paste on Enid's front view. She is complete, except that if you want her to stand up independently a substantial tab should be left below her feet which will slot into a wooden block below her feet (*see* p. 59). If this kind of stand is used, Enid can be removed from it and folded away in the paper wardrobe book I am going to describe in a moment. If you want to have her permanently on view, then

The Paper Doll

leave a tab at the feet, but cut out a square cardboard stand for her to rest on. Cut a slot in the centre of this stand to take the tab. Push it in and glue it in place with PVA adhesive.

Now you can turn your attention to cutting out the various outfits. Paste the paper (either traced from the book, or better still a xerox, so that you can make multiple copies) on to thin card. Cut round the outline of the dress, using a stencil cutter. Now give Enid a fitting. Place the dress or hat on top of her and move it around till it seems to be adjusted properly. Once you have it hanging properly, find out the position of the piece of MPT in the body of the doll which will make contact with the dress.

Figure 5. Front and back views of Costermonger's dress.

You can do this very easily by pushing about a piece of MPT on top of the dress until it stops moving, thus showing that the other "magnet" is right underneath. At this point push a needle through the dress at the exact spot to mark where it is. Turn the dress over, look for the needle hole and fix a slip of MPT on it. This piece of MPT should be bigger than the one let into the card. It should be, say, 1 cm (2/5 in.) square as opposed to the recessed slip which is 1 cm by $\frac{1}{2}$ cm. The larger size of MPT will make it much easier to find the spot where the dress makes contact with the doll, and also to ensure good adhesion. Glue the MPT slip to the *underside* of the dress with Uhu glue or other impact glue.

Figure 6. A golly outfit, with cut-a-way hole for face in front piece.

The Paper Doll

The minute you have finished making Enid and her dresses, you ought to think of constructing some hold-all in which they can be put away tidily. This will save them from getting lost or torn. One of the ways in which this can be done is to construct a framed picture, with MPT recessed into it here and there, to which Enid and the dresses may be stuck. This picture can then hang on the wall of the bedroom of Enid's owner. Old picture frames can be obtained very cheaply without the glass that was once in them. Buy an old frame without glass, and cut a piece of mounting board exactly the size to fit it. Cut recesses in the face of this piece of mounting board to take pieces of MPT on which Enid and the dresses will hang. These recesses must not be cut right through the board. It is enough to cut down into the sides of the recesses for about a millimetre, then lift out a layer of cardboard with the point of a craft knife.

Now decide what kind of picture you can use to paste on top of the mounting board. Think in terms of xeroxes of Victorian illustrations, such as a picture of a little girl's bedroom with a four poster bed, or a reproduction antique poster, or even a modern poster. An example of the kind of picture I have in mind is a poster that has recently been displayed by London transport. It shows a doll's house with the front opened and several dolls sitting about outside. Of course there is no reason why you should have to use a ready-made picture. You can paint a picture for yourself, or make up a collage. Alternatively use one of the many decorative papers I mentioned in the first chapter. Why not cover the board with a flower-flecked paper, then add collage of flower beds and cockle shells, so that Enid can become "Mary, Mary, Quite Contrary" in her garden?

Whatever form your picture takes, finish it neatly. Cut the picture (now pasted on the oblong of backing board) to size so that it fits exactly into the back of the frame. Anchor it in place there by driving special picture framer's nails (very small panel pins or framer's tingles) into the wood of the frame behind the edge of the back of the picture. Fix some fitment to the frame so that it can hang – two ring screws and a short length of cord will do for this – and hang the picture on the wall after you have driven in a proper picture hanging pin.

Another way of disposing of Enid and her wardrobe when they are not being played with is to tuck them away in a book which will fold shut. This book will be an oblong album. It will be made up on the same principles as those used to construct the Designoscope. It will have pieces of MPT inlaid into the inside of the covers so that the doll and the clothes can stick to them. There will be decorative papers on the covers, and also inside the covers as end papers. These end papers could, like the picture we have just talked about, be made up to look like the inside of a house, or its outside. Or they could be painted or collaged to look like a wardrobe. Wood grain paper will make a magnificent wardrobe.

The idea of storing paper dolls in books goes back to nineteenth-century France, when a publisher called Père Castor issued two books called, *The School*, and *The House*, each with its own population of dolls which dropped into slits in the book.

Putting dolls in books is certainly a way of disposing of them tidily and also knowing where they are. Ideally, the inside covers should have a shallow rim running round them to prevent doll and dresses becoming too crushed when they are put on the shelf. Ideally too, there should be a label on the back of the book. You can have a book for each family of dolls that you make. The "Colonial American Doll Family" could show the interior of a log cabin (in wood grain paper again) on one cover with mother spinning, helped by her daughter. The left-hand side of the book could represent Father's farm, with green plush paper to represent the grass, and dried grass or raffia collage to show the corn growing. Father, helped by his son, could be working in the fields.

A specialized type of paper figure is the military figurine. These figures can be furnished with concealed patches of MPT, like Enid, and various accessories can be attached to them by this means. The Chinese general whom I illustrate (Fig. 7) can either stand empty handed or grasp several kinds of shields. In order to have him holding a halberd, it is necessary to construct a separate arm attached to the halberd which will cover the existing arm completely.

Pictures made from backing board hung on the walls, which are not merely a way of disposing of paper dolls, can also be used as the background for exciting wall games. Wall toys are great space savers; they also do away with the troublesome business of tidying up a game at bedtime. Instead the game and all its

Figure 7. Chinese general with interchangeable MPT shields.

pieces can simply be left hanging on the wall, just as it stood when play was broken off.

There are so many possibilities for wall games and toys that you may well decide to extend and improve the list of examples I give. You may even decide not to rely entirely on old picture frames but begin to make your own. Quite small picture frame mouldings will be sufficiently robust to hold toys on a backing board base, as backing board is not very heavy. These frames can be cut on a wooden mitre board with a cabinet saw. The frame components can be cramped together and stuck with Evo-stik while a panel pin is knocked through each corner to hold it in place. On the back of the top segment of the frame, two "glass plates" (the trade name for brass triangles with holes to hold screws that fasten them to the frame and another hole that takes a screw holding them to the wall) can be attached. Once properly framed and hung, there is no chance of a wall toy coming adrift, no matter how much handling it takes. The plain wooden frame mouldings can be finished by varnishing them with clear lacquer, sanding them down and then varnishing them again. Once you have tired of a game, discard it and make another, of the right size to fit your existing frame. Don't forget that you can re-use your pieces of MPT from the old game.

Magnetic Chess and Draughts

So many types of MPT games are possible that it is difficult to know where to start. Probably the best thing to do is to begin with the simplest, magnetic chess and draughts (checkers). First cut out the board from backing board or other medium-thick cardboard. Mark out the right number of squares on the board; they should be an inch and a half (38 mm) in width. Allow a margin round the edge of the board, equal in width to the depth of the rim of the framing wood you are using. Cut square holes in the centre of each square. Do not cut right through, but only about half way through the board, leaving a layer of cardboard that can be levered out with the point of your knife. The holes you are cutting should be a centimetre square. Now cut 64 centimetre squares of MPT from a roll and put them to one side in a saucer, so that they do not get swept off the bench. Dip a brush in PVA adhesive and deposit a dab in each hole. Uhu can also be used for this purpose. Glue each square into its hole, making sure that each piece of tape sits flush in its hole.

Now you have to make up the chequered board for the chess or draughts. This can be plain black and white squares (made by cutting up surface paper, paper that is black on one side and white on the other) into one and a half inch squares. You need not use black and white. You may decide to construct the chessboard in decorative paper of two different colours or even metallic foil paper in two different metal foils, such as gold and silver.

You can now paste down the squares, a line at a time, using a ruler to make sure your lines of squares are straight avoiding overlaps, bumps over crumbs of paste or wrong alignments. Once you are sure that all the squares are correctly laid, and dry, finish the chess board by coating it with two coats of matt acrylic varnish. Alternatively you can spray it with artist's fixative. Most fixatives used nowadays are a synthetic cellulose solution which will protect the surface of your board while it is being played on. Alternatively you can cover the surface of the board completely

The Paper Doll

with any of the proprietary adhesive plastic coverings used for covering books.

When you are quite satisfied with your board, frame it and turn to making the chessmen or draughts (checkers). As these will have to take a lot of handling, I suggest you cut them, not from backing board, but from thin hardboard (Masonite), using a jeweller's saw or piercing saw for this purpose. Let us suppose that for our first chess set, we make one of the familiar Staunton pattern, the design almost all chessmen are made in. I have given illustrations of what the different pieces look like. (Fig. 8). If you want to begin by making a set of draughts (checkers) your task will be a lot easier. These are simply roundels and they can be cut out very simply by using a hole cutter in an electric drill. Most but not all hole cutters are supplied with a twist drill in the middle. I cut this in half and use the circular saw round the drill. Once you get used to it you will find that it can cut very neat discs out of harder material than hardboard.

When you have cut out the pieces, go over the edges with a needle file to make sure that they are smooth, or rub them down with an emery board. Paint the pieces with hardboard primer, allow them to dry, then paint or spray them carefully in two different colours to match your chess board squares.

As it would be difficult to cut square holes in the back of hardboard chessmen, just stick MPT squares to them with Uhu glue.

You can make up another kind of chessman, much more decorative and much more suitable for a flat board. These are based on Tibetan chess pieces (the originals are cut from human

Figure 8. Traditional chess pieces.

Figure 9. MPT Tibetan chessman.

bone!), and made up as flat slabs. Cut out thirty two cardboard squares from backing board, the same size as your chessboard squares. Round the corners very slightly. On the face of each square paste a square of paper on which you have pasted a xeroxed Tibetan chessman or one which you have traced or copied. As an alternative to pasting these chessmen on, just lay the paper on the card square with a square of mounting tissue in between, cover with a sheet of paper, and iron with a hot iron. The iron must be really hot to make the shellac of the mounting tissue melt and stick the paper to the card.

The Air Circus

The principles used in making up the chessboard can be applied to very many other projects. One of these is a toy for younger children — the Air Circus. A large oblong or square of backing board is prepared with as many pieces of MPT let into it as there are planes or other aircraft in the circus. These pieces are let into the part of the picture that is going to be "the air", while in addition there are a number of pieces let into the bottom of the picture, which is the landing field, so that while all the aircraft can be airborne at once, there is still plenty of room to position some of them on the field. Once enough MPT squares have been cut

The Paper Doll

into the background of the picture, the whole surface of the air circus picture is covered with a sheet of art paper. The picture shows the sky, clouds and a grass runway. These are rendered in paint (preferably solid colour paint like poster paint) or possibly collage.

The buildings which I have suggested in my illustrations can be painted on the card or made separately from it and stuck down. The latter treatment certainly has to be followed with the hangar and balloon shed, which can be used as working models. They are really narrow slots in the cardboard into which most of the aircraft can be pushed for storage (Fig. 10). To get the aircraft out of the hangar, all that is necessary to do is to slide a piece of MPT (or better still a small magnet such as an Eclipse magnet) along the back of the picture to draw them out. The buildings (*see* Fig. 11) should be painted with gouache colour, with perhaps a little detail added with a mapping pen and Indian ink. Small squares of mirror paper are stuck here and there on the window frames to suggest the sunlight flashing from the panes on a fine sunny day. The whole toy should look like a scene from the 1930s.

The planes which I have suggested are also rather old fashioned (Fig. 12), though there is no reason why they should not be models of today. They should be brightly painted. It is often possible to find pictures of ready-made aircraft which can

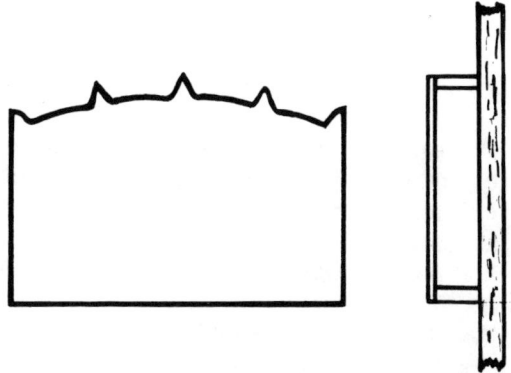

Figure 10. Hangar or balloon shed made from a shallow box, parallel to the baseboard, into which to slot aircraft.

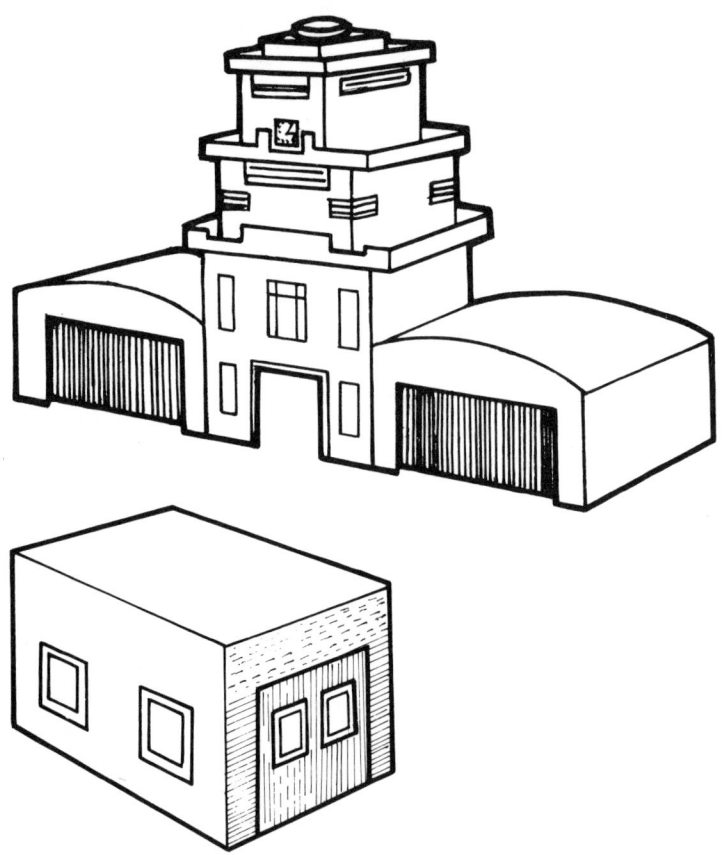

Figure 11. Airport buildings: control tower and fire station/ambulance depot.

be simply stuck to a backing board or mounting board backing. In Britain there are various firms which own advertising dirigibles which are much publicized. Magazine advertisements and posters are another source for pictures for ready-made planes. However constructed, planes, balloons and helicopters must have a piece of MPT stuck to them on the underside. A small child will find plenty to do in bringing the planes out of their hangar (using a thin piece of card to push them out from the other end if he is too small to take the picture off the wall), finding a place for them to hover in the sky, arranging for the descent of the parachutists and the ascent of the balloonists and placing the fire-engine and ambulance on the runway – just in case.

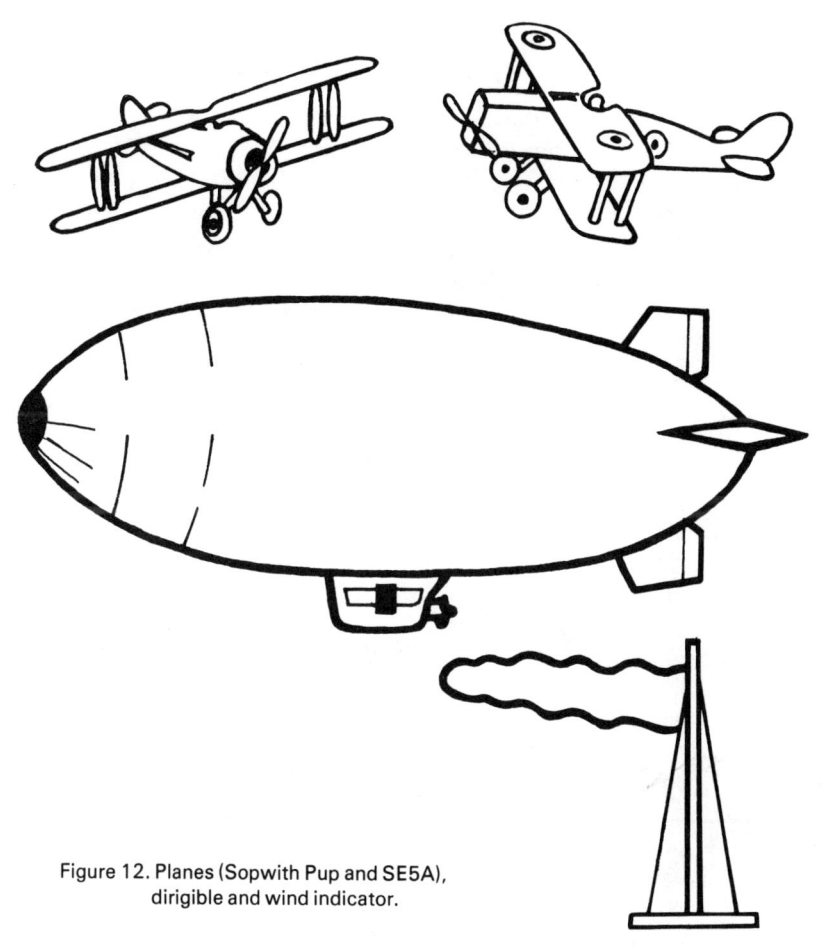

Figure 12. Planes (Sopwith Pup and SE5A), dirigible and wind indicator.

It is easy to turn this toy into a game. Divide the aircraft and other equipment into two teams and throw dice to see whose turn it is to move a plane. The player who gets all his team airborne first wins.

To make the game more exiting, the wind changes every four moves (this is indicated by changing the direction of the drogue on the wind indicator, which swivels). Planes can only take off into the direction of the wind, though of course helicopters and balloons can rise whatever the wind conditions. The experienced player will then try to divide his team so that he has as near an equal number of aircraft as possible facing down the runway in two different directions.

Deep Diving Game

The MPT game in greatest contrast to the air circus is the Deep Diving Game. An impressive-looking ocean deep is created by pasting a sheet of green mat metallic foil paper, or deep green cellophane, over the prepared MPT patches. At the top a line of rolling breakers topped with white foam gives way to a blue sky with fleecy white clouds. Right at the bottom is the sea bed, represented by an irregularly undulating bank of sand. The clouds are made by laying tufts of cotton wool on good quality white drawing paper and spraying them with blue poster paint. The tufts are removed when the paint has dried and white clouds are left on the blue ground.

A few dried plants and grasses, pressed flat, can be pasted below the cellophane. These dried ornamental grasses, which suggest the great tangles of weed in the ocean depths, can be bought from John Galt toyshops.

At the bottom of the sea is a sunken galleon, a treasure ship whose riches both sides are trying to acquire. Whichever side reaches the sea bottom first is held to be the winner. Both sides have diving vessels on the surface, and both have to send down a midget submarine to attach a line to the wreck. The galleon has broken into two halves and there is one half beneath each vessel. Only when the line is in place can each salvage team send down its diver. A killer whale, a giant squid and a mammoth shark, all of which move sideways but at different levels, are operated by a third player to hinder the work of salvage, and as an added complication, although there is some cargo in each half of the wreck (slotted into a shallow cardboard box like the aeroplane hangars), nobody is sure till the last moment which half holds the treasure.

Air Battle Games

Another air game, and one in which several players can join, is the multiple dog-fight of the First World War days. At this time, the ability of a fighter to climb above an opponent meant at least the likelihood of a victory. The object of the game is for the various players to get their fighters to climb up ladders of pieces of MPT positioned in the board until they reach the top, when they can begin to move sideways, in order to top an enemy fighter, not necessarily the one with which they were originally

The Paper Doll

paired. Needless to say the ladder of MPT pieces is concealed by the picture (a real aerial photograph?) covering the backing board.

Another war game utilizes the tendency of the magnetically tacked on pieces to fall off the board occasionally. Make up a tall oblong of backing board. This oblong is not intended to be framed, instead it is free standing, resting in a substantial wood stand, a block of wood of sufficient length and size to hold it, which has a slot made by a wood saw down the middle. Into this slot the bottom of the cardboard is fitted. Supported as it is only at the bottom, the backing board can "wobble" considerably, which is necessary for the purposes of the game.

On the board is painted with gouache paint a night sky, deep blue, with some lighter clouds, a thin crescent moon and a few twinkling stars (which can be made in mirror paper or silver foil metallic paper). At the bottom of the board the earth is indicated with a few clumps of woods and bushes, while one or two gleaming metal gun barrels, emerging from the branches indicate the position of an anti-aircraft battery.

Across the backing board are laid two "trails" of MPT which cross the picture from left to right. One, substantially higher than the other, is for the bombers, while the one lower down is for the fighters. These trails are made from patches of MPT laid about an inch apart. One player in the game (who represents the attacking aircraft) sits on the picture side of the board. His task is to push the bombers and fighters across the picture and along the trails, from one MPT square to another, moving in each move one length of a fighter or bomber. To push the planes he uses a wooden pusher. The planes are cut from backing board pasted over with the picture of a plane (acquired ready made from some magazine), stuck down with PVA and subsequently cut from the backing board with a piercing saw. The completed plane is covered with a piece of blue cellophane to simulate its nighttime appearance. Needless to say a square of MPT is stuck to the underside.

The other player, who represents the anti-aircraft battery, sits on the blank side of the board. He is allowed to hit the top of the wooden stand once with a small wooden hammer after any move has been made. Any fighters or bombers dislodged from the MPT trails belong to him, but if they land directly on the bat-

Figure 13. MPT Climbing Game.

tery he loses the game.

The purpose of the game is to fly over the board a squadron of bombers and fighters (the squadron need not be full strength). One of the decisions that the players will have to make for themselves is whether it is safer to pass planes over singly or in mass formation.

The Climbing Game
This chapter might well end with another and more peaceful game, one which tries to reproduce some of the conditions of real life in play. One of the difficulties in mountaineering is finding your next hand and foothold. This problem has suggested the climbing game I am going to describe. Cardboard figures of two

The Paper Doll

mountaineers, each roped to the other by a short length of thread, have to move up the ladders built of MPT on a cliff face. The cliff face need not look terribly authentic. Rough-stone doll's house paper does quite well. To make the game more difficult some of the ladders are false trails, ending in dead ends or in sideways moves which lose time for the climbers. The players throw dice to decide who will have first choice of the different numbered routes. Eventually these routes may become well known to the players, whereupon a new board can be constructed, or the old one reversed, as there is no obvious top or bottom to the cliff. Each player moves once each go, and he can only move one of his figures the length of the rope that ties it to the following figure. The first one to reach the top wins.

3. Papier-mâché Toys

No book on paper toys ought to omit papier mâché (a French term which means just "pulped paper"). The modern French name for this medium is not so accurately descriptive as its old one, also French, which was *carton pierre*, or "stone cardboard", for papier mâché really is paper processed so that it is rock hard. Papier mâché is a godsend to the paper toymaker because in the first place it enables him to escape from the flat shapes in which so many of his toys are built, and really become three-dimensional. Then too it lets him use up all the left overs and dispose of all these pieces of waste cardboard and paper that he is always acquiring by putting them to some good use. But the biggest attraction of papier mâché to the toymaker is perhaps its centuries-old tradition as a medium for toys. Even nowadays probably more toys are made from papier mâché than any other kind of paper. In Mexico alone millions of toys are turned out for little Mexicans on occasions such as Christmas and All Souls' Day. The latter is a festival little observed in the Protestant world but in many Catholic countries it is *the* most important festival, because it is the Festival of the Dead, who in a poor family may well outnumber the living. The very intricate and to our eye, macabre, toys of Mexican children (which on All Souls' Day often take the form of skeletons) show just what can be done with this splendid material. At the other end of the world, in Japan, chunky, solid-looking toys in papier mâché look completely different, but are just as successful as designs. I have not done singing the praises of papier mâché yet. It is the cheapest form of paper toy material, because it can be made from old newspapers, which can be obtained free. It is the only paper medium for toys which admits of quick and easy moulding. So it

Figure 15. Skeleton framework and sculpted Mexican Christmas festival toy.

Sculptured Toys

Papier mâché is best applied to the project required straight away. Even if stored as I have suggested, it will work best when it is newly mixed. Left too long, it has a tendency to become crumbly. While still moist it is a natural sculptor's material, just like clay. As it dries extremely hard and can be filed and sawed to correct any early mistakes in modelling, it is ideal for sculptured toys. Elaborate versions of these could be, like the Mexican festival toy that I illustrate, real statues built up on a wire armature. Much easier to make is the head, either for a puppet, or for a doll. The head is built up on a cardboard tube. This you can either find ready-made or build yourself by wrapping paper round a piece of wooden dowelling, three quarters of an inch (19mm) thick and about five or six inches (140mm) long. Paste the paper with PVA adhesive as you go and you will soon have a stout cardboard tube. As the foundation for this tube, use a piece of waxed paper so that you can slip the tube off the wooden former. Now taper the ends of the cylinder in by cutting three "Vee" cuts in the cylinder with a craft tool at one end. Pull the pointed ends of the top of the cylinder together and wrap them round with strips of paper pasted in PVA adhesive so that you turn the paper cylinder from an open tube to a closed tube. To model a head on to the cylinder, just wrap one end round with pieces of well frayed string and paste them in place with PVA. Let the PVA adhesive dry, then begin to smear on fairly moist papier mâché so that it integrates itself with the ends of the string. Mould the ball of papier mâché with boxwood modelling tools so that it takes on the features of a face. When it is finished, stand it upright on a piece of dowel clamped into the vice of your workbench. Sand down the completed head, fill in any crevices with fresh papier mâché, allow it to dry, then sand it again. Prime the head, then paint it with Humbrol enamels.

What kind of a head should you model? The traditional doll's head of the Victorian type which has now become popular once more and is being reproduced in porcelain could be one project. There is no need to model the hair. This can be added much more effectively in the shape of a nylon wig, cut from long tufted nylon fabric.

There is no need for your first head to be a doll's. Why not make up a set of glove puppets with your fingers manipulating the head through the cylinder? Just add a costume to the doll by stitching it on the cylinder below the neck.

One of the virtues of papier mâché is that it is very easy to mould in wooden moulds which can be cut by the modeller. Moulding not merely makes possible toys that require a number of pieces, it also enables the craftsman to create large numbers of papier mâché toys that can be sold at a school fair or craft fair.

The Daruma or Japanese Tumbler

The simplest toy is the best to begin with when it comes to moulding, and no toy could possibly be simpler than the daruma or Japanese tumbler. This folk art toy, which has been produced for centuries in Japan, represents a hermit whose austerities were so severe that his legs withered away. Weighted at the bottom, he will bob up whichever way he is pushed. Japanese have the odd habit of producing this toy without eyes. The eyes (either round or slanted) are then dotted in with a brush and Indian ink by the customer himself. The eye dotting is quite a ceremony and is usually reserved for some major or minor triumph, such as passing an examination.

The principles for making the Daruma are much the same as

Figure 16. Design for Daruma.

for any other moulded toy. Begin by checking that you have a piece of wood sufficient to contain the moulded toy, then saw the block of wood in two and plane the faces of both halves. Next draw the outline of the toy. It is a help in doing this if you draw a half profile only, that is one side of the toy (provided that it is, like the Daruma, symmetrical). Trace the half profile twice on to a piece of paper with tracing paper so that you have an absolutely symmetrical outline of the toy. Place the two halves of your prepared block of wood in a vice and clamp them together. Now drill right through the block in the top right hand corner. This hole will let you line up the two halves of the block when you come to use it as a mould.

It is essential that the two scooped out halves of the mould meet exactly. One way of ensuring that this happens is to cut out a paper pattern for the Daruma on thin paper, hinged in the middle by a small piece of paper that is not cut. Slip a piece of waxed paper between the two halves of the pattern, then paste both halves with PVA adhesive and place them between the two halves of the block of wood, which should be laid exactly on top of one another. Leave under a weight for some time. The two halves of the paper pattern can now be slit apart with a sharp knife and the places for the two halves of the mould will be marked out so that they correspond exactly. Go round the edge of the paper pattern on each half with a Rapidograph pen just in order to ensure that you have a clear outline.

Cutting a wooden mould is a little like making a spoon – you have to start in the middle. First, though, cut round the outline with a sharp stencil cutter or other small craft knife. Cut right into

Figure 17. A. Mould incorrectly cut. B. Mould correctly cut.

the centre of the mould using an Xacto knife with a large size handle and a gouge, or a carpenter's gouge if you have one. Keep cutting down towards the centre, never work outwards. When you have done what you can with a gouge, take a router, such as an Xacto router, and rout round the inside bowl shape you are cutting till it is as smooth as you can make it. Work with the grain, not against it. Now take some coarse sandpaper and roll it into a spill with a pointed end, like a pencil. Rub this round the inside of your mould until it is as smooth as you can make it. Follow with medium sandpaper and finally complete the job with fine sandpaper. When you have got the inside as smooth as you can with sandpaper, polish it with the rounded end of a boxwood modelling tool. You will find that rubbing with this tool smooths the inside of the mould very considerably. The mould now only needs oiling to be ready for use. Rub over the whole mould with linseed oil and rub in as much as you can with a cloth. Use boiled linseed oil for this purpose. Now lay out both halves and fill them up with linseed oil. Leave overnight. The mould will need constant wiping down with a wet cloth and re-oiling from time to time.

Mix up some papier mâché and fill the mould with it, with a palette knife. Push some lead shot into the bottom half of the papier mâché and fill so that it weights the toy. Bring the two halves of the mould together. Push a nail or screw into the hole that goes right through the mould and clip it in the vice so that it is brought together under pressure. Leave overnight for the papier mâché to dry. In the morning tip the daruma out of the mould, tapping the wall of the mould with a plastic tipped hammer if it shows a tendency to retain the casting. There should be no lead shot showing on the outside as lead is poisonous and must never be allowed to get into children's hands. Smooth off the flash line and set the daruma aside to dry. This is

Figure 18. A Japanese *Inu-hariko*.

a gradual process and it can be accelerated by leaving the casting in a warm room such as an airing cupboard. When the toy is completely dry you can trim off anything that still remains of the flash line, and sand down the papier mâché, just as though it were a piece of wood. Finish with fine sandpaper, apply priming paint, then two coats of white paint and decorate in the colour scheme you prefer. If you are making a large number of daruma tumblers for a craft fair, it helps to apply the white coats with a spray and to have each member of the family painting a particular part of the toy.

The practice obtained from making the daruma can be applied to making another very popular Japanese folk toy, which I also illustrate, a jolly dog called *Inu-hariko*, which is a good luck present. Cut the mould so that the ears are moulded together, then when the toy is dry, separate the ears by cutting a "vee" with a craft knife and a file.

Ninepins

An obvious development of the art of making moulded toys is to make moulded sets of toys, such as ninepins. There is very little that need be added to the information that the reader already has to start him off making ninepins. I give an illustration of a shape for these toys which was evolved in Ancient Egypt. No doubt, like the Japanese toys, it owes some of its success to the fact that it is a design that has evolved as a result of trial and error. Cut a mould for the ball that is going to knock down the ninepins in the same block as the ninepin itself so that they can

Figure 19. An Ancient Egyptian ninepin.

be made together. When the ninepins are all dry, stand them on a sheet of sandpaper and rub them round in a circular motion, one by one, to ensure that they stand correctly.

It is not too difficult a step to move from the constriction of the mould to the freedom of a freestanding, hand-modelled toy. So long as you have a wooden base, and an armature of the type I illustrate (in Fig. 15) there is no limit, save your own perseverance to the elaboration and artistry which you lavish on a special toy of this sort.

4. War Gaming in Paper

A few weeks ago I was reminded of the strong connection that once existed between toy soldiers, as they were called in my youth, military miniatures, as they are now, and paper. I was looking at a coloured printed sheet containing file after file of French infantrymen on the march. They were all dressed in the blue and red uniform of the French army, as worn by soldiers between the Franco-Prussian War and the Great War. The sheet was what was called in France an *image d'Epinal*. It had probably been issued by one of the well known publishing firms who specialized in paper toys, such as the *Imagerie Pellérin*. It was not for sale in a toy shop, though, but in one of those antiquarian booksellers, called *bouquinistes*, who keep their books in hutches fastened to the granite walls of the *quais* along the bank of the Seine, in Paris, near the *Île Saint Louis*. The sheet of soldiers was a valuable antique, and was priced accordingly. Even if it had not been too expensive, I should never have had the heart to cut up such a beautiful piece of traditional folk art and put it to the destination for which it was originally intended, being pasted to a cardboard backing, and cut up with scissors to make individual soldiers, or groups of soldiers.

At one time these paper soldiers must have been very common all over Europe, for it was only a few well-to-do children who could, like young Winston Churchill, own whole regiments of metal soldiers. The toy soldiers made up from the printed sheets were of course "flats", that is, silhouettes, not rounded figures, but children of the time were used to such toys, because many lead soldiers were made up as "flats" as well, and they are still being made. Paper soldiers were, and are, much more true to life than those commonly made in the round, because they were all designed by artists and looked extremely realistic. The French infantrymen at whom I was looking were so full of dash and verve that I felt that I could almost hear the tramp of their boots. Paper is such a deceptive material that it has even deceived real soldiers in time of warfare. Once during the sixteenth century, a Japanese general called Hideyoshi was besieging a castle, whose garrison held out stubbornly. Then, overnight, Hideyoshi had a castle the same size as the one which he was besieging constructed right beside it. The morale of the garrison was so weakened by this incredible feat that they surrendered right away. Only after they marched out of their stronghold did they discover that the enemy "castle" was really made from paper.

Although you can no longer buy *images d'Epinal*, because they are no longer published and only turn up as occasional, and expensive, antique items, it is very easy to construct your own army, along with all the transport, war material, fortifications and scenery needed to fight a war game, for the price of just one antique print. Nor, when you have constructed your army, need it suffer the fate of the *image d'Epinal* soldiers, which was to become torn, and grubby, or lose arms and legs.

All you need to make splendidly authentic military models is a master print, the use of a photocopying machine, some waste cardboard, PVA adhesive or cold water paste, a piercing saw and some fine sawblades, a length of wooden batten or slotted framewood to support your figures, a little matt acrylic varnish, a paste brush and a paint brush. If you so prefer, the figures you make can be in black and white, but if you want them coloured, it is very simple to colour them yourself, using good quality water colours for this purpose. "Instant" colour can be added, if so desired, by sticking down Transeal, or any other adhesive colour sheet, on to the black and white figures, then cutting round the outline with a craft knife and cutting out spaces for the face and hands. Having briefly indicated how colour can be applied, I shall, for the rest of this chapter, talk about black and white figures only. They are the quickest and easiest kind of model soldier to make and they are quite suitable for all war gaming purposes.

War Gaming in Paper

Making the Models

To make paper military miniatures you must have a master print which can be xeroxed to produce copies which will be made up into soldier figures. In fact, as you will need several different kinds of figures to create an army, you need several master prints. The best master prints to copy from are those made in black and white, such as wood cut engravings in old books, or black and white draughtsman's illustrations — the kind drawn in pen and ink which have clear, definite and black lines on a white background. Do not try to xerox colour. It will not reproduce well enough for the purpose you want, even if you xerox it on one of those sophisticated machines which allows for copying of coloured originals.

Where will you find master prints for your soldiers? Surprisingly, the answer is "everywhere". While I smoked, I used occasionally to purchase expensive cigarettes called "Abdullahs". On the black and white packet was a beautiful representation of an Egyptian and a Sudanese soldier of the period round about 1900. Wrappings and advertisements will provide lots of originals to copy — there is a lot of military art in advertising nowadays. So too will many illustrations in contemporary magazines, particularly those magazines devoted to modelling and to war gaming. Old newspapers, which can be borrowed and photocopied on the spot in big libraries, provide a wealth of original models. Papers such as the *Illustrated London News* covered all important wars, such as the American Civil War, for example, and the articles by "our own correspondent" were beautifully illustrated.

The best and most reliable source for master prints is your own library. Get into the habit of browsing over old book stalls and barrows, and be alert for the tattered volume — perhaps an odd one of a set, and therefore going cheap — that will provide you with a lot of military material. Supposing you were lucky enough to pick up either Volume I or Volume II of Sir Henry Morton Stanley's *How I found Livingstone*, you would be set up for life with all the material you needed for a war game based on nineteenth-century Africa. The illustrations would provide you with plenty of explorers, porters, gun boats, maxim guns, palm trees, *bomas*, tribesmen, thorn forests, grass huts, wild beasts and so on.

Sift through your material with two ideas in mind. Your figures have to be all the same scale, or approximately so, and they have to be all from the same period, if they are to look authentic. It is much better not to decide on a scale, and then look round for illustrations that fit it. Instead, look at your illustrations and decide what is the size of figure that most commonly appears in them. The size you choose is a matter for your preference, but once you have chosen, stick to that size, unless you decide to branch out on a new period or country to model from.

Old "flat" figures, the flat model soldiers in lead that we are going to try to imitate in paper, were almost always modelled side-on. The details of the figure showed up on both sides. In the figures we are going to make, details of features and armour will only appear on the front. "Flats" were almost invariably modelled so that they were in profile – though there were exceptions to this rule. I suggest you vary the stance of your figures and model some in profile and some full face. This is what I have done in my castle scene where full-face figures appear on the ramparts and profile figures below them.

One of the fascinating aspects of paper military soldiering is the speed with which the soldiers can be produced. It would take months to develop a piece of authentic source material, such as a contemporary illustration showing Grant's seizure of the Round Tops before the Battle of Gettysburg, into plastic or metal figures. With paper it is a matter of minutes. Whole groups of soldiers can be modelled and attached to one stand (as with the old metal flats) and it is also possible to reproduce large sections of the scenery of the battlefield and mount it for scenic presentation. With regard to scenery, here it is possible to relax the rules of scale slightly. If a farmhouse, or some other landscape accessory stands some little way back from the battlefield, it can be made smaller, on the assumption that it is seen in perspective.

Xeroxing only costs pennies, but pennies add up to pounds, and if you are creating a large army, make sure that you get full value for your money. If there is any part of an illustration that you are reproducing that you do not want to use, fill in the dead ground with figures that you do want to include. Have these ready cut out, either singly or in groups, so that they can be placed on the parts of the book or sheet that you are copying. Try

Figure 20. Paper soldiers clash in front of a castle.

to photocopy as much of what you want, and as little of what you don't want, with every exposure.

Mounting the Pieces
Once you have xeroxed a sufficient number of figures with which to begin, choose some cardboard about an eighth of an inch thick. It can either be mounting board, that you buy or waste cardboard. For many of the examples that I illustrate I have used cardboard that I get free with photographs sent to me through the post, as packing.

Once you have assembled before you some cardboard; a bowl of flour paste or a jar of PVA (which should be slightly diluted); a large and a small paste brush; a bowl of water for washing the paste brushes when they become clogged with paste; a clean rag for wiping the brushes dry; a bone folder for rubbing down the pasted paper; a clean duster for the same purpose; and a stack of waste paper on which to paste, you are ready to begin.

The pasting pad of waste paper is made up beforehand by cutting a large newspaper down the fold with a bookbinder's knife. Each sheet is then laid on top of another, in a stack. Paper to be pasted is laid, face down, on the top sheet and pasted. After the pasting has been done the top sheet is thrown away into a waste bin, so that no wet paste is left to adhere where it is not wanted. The carbon used to print xeroxes is very pervasive stuff, and it does no harm to wash your hands from time to time during the pasting process to make sure that none of it is sticking to your fingers.

Cutting out the xeroxed sheets before they are stuck down demands a certain amount of thought. Cut so as to allow a margin around your figure, but not too large a margin. This will help to economize your cardboard. Many illustrations have a caption underneath which is useful for your purpose. A figure in a text book on armour for example may have underneath the caption: "Soldier, (Sloane MS. 346 c. 1280)". This caption should be cut out separately and attached to the *back* of the figure you are going to make. Documentation of this sort is useful for conveying authenticity to your models. It is also very useful for sorting out figures into the right decade for a particular battle, as well as for distinguishing between officers and other ranks. If there is no useful caption to provide you with the information you want, try adding it in the form of a typed label (preferably typed on a typewriter with a very legible face, such as an IBM) or add the information in Letraset. If labels of this sort do nothing else, they act as a sort of potted textbook on military history for your benefit.

Lay the xeroxed picture face down on a waste sheet, and paste it rapidly, starting by brushing paste into the centre and then directing your brush strokes outwards. Now turn the xerox, pasted side up, lay it aside for a moment, and rapidly paste the cardboard. If your xerox is a large one, press the two ends of the pasted side together so that they meet. Do this only if you are using cold water paste, as if you have pasted the sheet with PVA you will be unable to separate the two ends of the sheet. Now place the pasted xerox on the cardboard and rub it down gently, using a soft duster and a bone folder for this purpose. Look out for small lumps of paste which have not been stirred into the mixture properly. These will stand out as unsightly lumps on the pasted-down xerox once it is in place if they are not removed at this stage. Peel back the sheet and pick out the lumps with the point of a bookbinder's knife. Avoid smudging so far as you are able. The paste brush may pick up some of the black from the surface of xeroxes. Console yourself with the fact that if there are black smudges on the face of the completed figure, they can be painted out with Chinese white.

Once you have covered the *face* of the cardboard with your xerox, paste the *back* of it with a sheet of waste white paper. This is to "draw" the cardboard in the opposite direction and prevent it warping towards the xerox side. Once both sides have been pasted leave the completed board aside to dry, under wax-coated archivists' paper (if you can get it) with a flat board on top and a weight on top of the board. Allow a day and night for flour paste to dry out, a few hours if you are using PVA. When it has dried, examine the cardboard for any signs of warping. If the board is not flat, press it again. Go on doing this until you have a completely flat piece of cardboard. It is a great help in achieving this flatness if the waste paper that you paste on the back is the same thickness as the xerox paper. There is another feature of the pasting process that must be mentioned. Whereas cold water paste merely pastes the paper down to the board, PVA strengthens the cardboard, making it tougher and stiffer as it is incorporated with it. For this reason cardboard figures made with PVA are tougher and more resilient than those pasted with cold water paste.

Some care is needed with the pasting process, and even when a double sheet is pasted on cardboard it does not always become flat immediately, as I have said. For this reason photographers and other workers in the visual arts usually prefer to *dry mount* their prints. They take a sheet of dry mounting tissue, which is tissue paper coated on both sides with shellac, and place it between the print to be mounted and the cardboard. Just to hold it in place while it is being positioned, they lay the tissue on the back of the print and touch it with a really hot iron. This holds the tissue till it can be placed on the board and ironed all over. A sheet of paper is placed over the print to be mounted. The dry mounting process might prove extremely useful to you if you had a large number of prints to mount at once or, if you did not want them to get wet by pasting them because you had coloured them with water colour and were afraid of the colour running.

Cutting out the Pieces
Whereas the Victorian schoolboy who had bought an *image d'Epinal* print and pasted it down on cardboard was faced with the near impossible task of cutting out the cardboard soldiers from the completed board with a pair of scissors, you have a very much easier task ahead of you.

All you need to cut out your figures is a jeweller's saw (or piercing saw) with a fine blade (together with an adequate stock of replacements if the blade breaks), a sawing pin (a small length of board with a "vee" cut at one end, which is clamped to your bench or worktable with a G clamp), and a small drill. The drill can either be an ordinary twist drill, or an Archimedean drill that you can work with one hand for making holes in the interior sections of the board that have to be cut out. Equipped with tools like these, cutting out a cardboard soldier is no more difficult a task than any other piece of fretwork. Curiously enough, I do not recall anyone ever having employed a saw for this purpose.

You are now ready to begin cutting the figure. The board is clamped at right angles to your bench, with the "vee" towards you. You will hold the cardboard sheet on this "vee" so that the saw blade works up and down in the centre. Instead of trying to move *yourself* round the figure while you cut it out, you will instead *turn the figure round* so that you are always sawing in one direction only — the one that is most convenient for yourself. If you are working on a large sheet of cardboard, you may find it more convenient to subdivide it into sections before you begin cutting out the individual figures.

Before you begin cutting out the figures, study them carefully. Do you want to cut round the whole outline of the figure? Obviously you do not, because you must leave a tab at the bottom which will subsequently be slotted into a wooden batten. This tab should stretch for at least half an inch (12.7 mm) beneath the base of the figure. Nor, apart from the tab, need you cut strictly to the figure's silhouette. If you are cutting out a cannon, for example, why not include the smoke cloud that billows from its mouth as well as the barrel of the gun, its carriage and wheels? If you are sawing out a ship, you will certainly want to include some of the waves on which it floats, while you might well decide to include some of the background of scurrying cloud behind it as well. This decision will enable you to side-step doing a

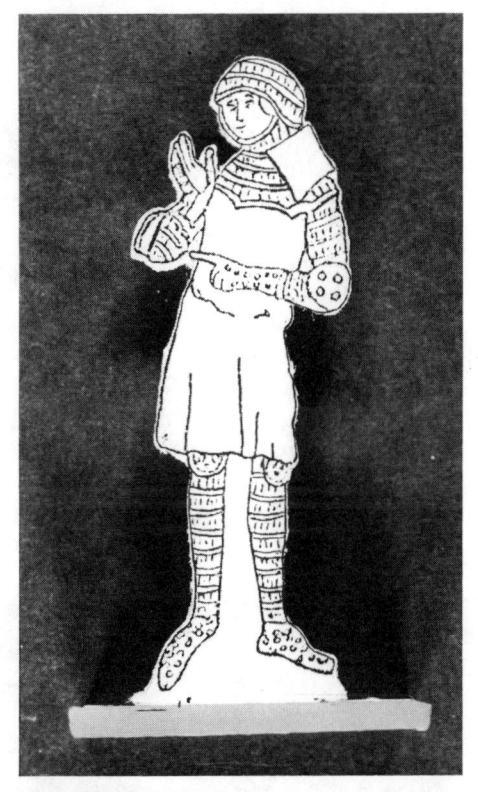

Figure 21. Standing figure with wooden batten.

lot of difficult sawing and cutting out detached flying pennants, sailors in the rigging and so forth. In fact the more complex a military miniature is, the less you need detach it from its background. Even if you are cutting a fairly simple figure, say a soldier with a lance, you may decide to leave a tie between the lance and the soldier, so as to save a fairly fragile part, such as the lance, from being broken off in handling.

Once you have decided what to saw out and what to leave, mark the parts which are to be removed with coloured crayon, just in case you saw through the wrong part by mistake. Now drill holes in the interior parts that have to be removed. Saw out these first, by loosening your sawblade at the top of the frame, pushing it through the hole from beneath, tightening it once more, and sawing out the inside section. Often a few extra drill holes, placed at strategic points inside the interior section, will help your task. It is important to cultivate a straight-up-and-down motion with the saw, making even strokes. If you make jerky, irregular strokes you will produce a saw-toothed edge to the cut.

Once you have sawn out all the interior sections, do the outside silhouette. Keep the tab till last, but do not saw the bottom, where it is going to rest in the wooden slot of the batten. Instead, once you have completed the figure, lay the cut out on a cutting board, and cut the bottom straight with a straight edge and craft knife.

The cut edges of the figure should be reasonably smooth. If they are not, trim them up by smoothing the edge with needle files. If you still have a ragged edge, paint the whole edge of the figure with diluted PVA adhesive applied with a small brush and

Figure 22. Military miniature positioned so that the horse appears to rear up.

War Gaming in Paper

work over the edge of the figure with a boxwood modelling tool or a bone folder till it is smooth. This treatment will not merely smooth it down now, but it will prevent the edge fraying in the future while the figure is being handled. Label the back of the figure with its identifying label. The more attractive and legible this looks, the better. Do not forget that in a "battle" you will be looking at the backs of your figures and your opponent at their fronts. Now you can seal the whole figure, preventing it from becoming dirty while it is being handled, by coating it with diluted matt acrylic varnish. As an alternative, spray the whole figure with artist's fixative, or paint it with water colour varnish. The latter finish is, however, best used in conjunction with water colours if you decide to paint the figure.

Do not fall into the same trap that I did when I was experimenting with backing materials. Instead of using cardboard I decided I would use plasticard for my military miniatures, only to find that it gave a very fuzzy edge when cut by a saw, and that it was virtually impossible to make the paper used for xeroxing stick to it and not peel off.

Mounting the figure is a very simple affair. Much the best way is to buy wood strip in the form of a square batten that is already grooved. This will usually be available in a size of about three quarters of an inch (19 mm) square. If you want a smaller batten you may have to make it yourself out of wood strip, half an inch (12.7 mm) by a quarter of an inch (6.3 mm) and groove it with a cabinet saw. You can widen the saw groove by cutting into it with a wood gouge. From whatever size of batten it is cut, the mount should be longer than the base of the cardboard figure by at least a quarter of an inch on either side. Make up a simple jig to cut your battens if you are doing a large number at a time. Otherwise mark them up with a try square and scratch the edge with a metal stylus. The squarer the ends of the batten look, once the mount is made up, the better will be the appearance of the mount. I cut my mounts with an Xacto saw, or with a jeweller's saw.

Once you have cut the mount, rub it over with fine sandpaper. Paint the wood with polyurethane wood filler, rub it down, then varnish it with clear polyurethane varnish, before rubbing it down again. If you want a light coloured base to the figure, omit the filler. Now give the mount a final coat of varnish. No amount

Figure 23. This paper military miniature is temporarily held in place on its stand with a blob of Blu-tack.

of handling should now be able to affect it.

When you have got the mount finished to your satisfaction, check to see if the groove is deep enough to take the tab at the base of the figure. It should be at least a quarter of an inch deep. Offer up the figure to the groove. If it sits slackly, it can be wedged by a small slip of cardboard. To cement the figure into the groove run a *small* amount of Evo-stik or some other white carpenter's glue into the groove, position the tab at the base of the figure in it and hold it in place with a blob of Bostik Blu-tack (a tacky artist's putty that can be used again and again) until the glue has dried.

Military figurines do not have to have a wooden stand. They can be slotted into a hole that has been cut with a jeweller's saw

War Gaming in Paper 61

in an oblong piece of cardboard, just big enough to receive the tab, and then glued in place with PVA. Alternately they can be given an "invisible" support, consisting of a square tab of cardboard slightly smaller than the whole figure, glued to its back at right angles with PVA adhesive. The cardboard tab is more the orthodox kind of mounting that you would expect to find on a military figurine. It does however take up much more room than a wooden batten. The batten also makes it possible to store the soldiers, by the hundred if need be, without fear of their being damaged. A cabinet is constructed in which the shelves are slotted. The figures are simply pushed along the slots in the shelves so that they hang head down, suspended by the base.

Paper soldiers have several marked advantages over other kinds of military miniatures. They are so light that they can be subjected to real missiles, and be knocked down without suffering any damage. It is not possible to do this with metal or plastic soldiers.

Conversions can be effected very simply. All that it is necessary to do to convert a figure is to alter the master print. If your

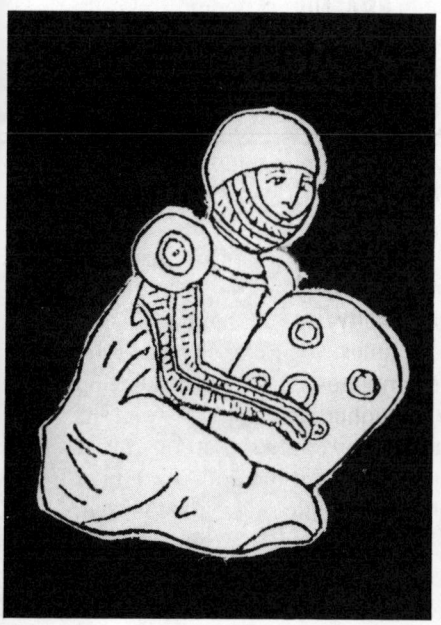

Figure 24. A free-standing figure with "invisible" mounting.

master print is a soldier without a shield and you want him to have a shield, just cut a shield out from some other print and lay it on the master while it is being xeroxed. The soldier, now equipped with a shield, becomes in turn the master for a whole series of copies. All sorts of additions can be made in this way: an arm holding a lance or pennon, a helmet and so forth. It is very easy to undertake quite complicated conversions such as mounting a rider on a horse.

Nor need the paper war gamer be tied down to such prints as he can find. There is no reason why the modeller should not strike out boldly and construct his own figures by simply drawing them on good quality white paper with a Rapidograph or other draughtsman's pen. This method leaves a drawing which will be almost identical in tone with book illustrations.

Battlefield Accessories
Not just soldiers, but all the accessories of the "battlefield" can be made up from paper, indeed it would be out of keeping with the figures to make them from any other material. The scenery will be all invisibly mounted, with a buttress propping them up from behind, pasted to the back of the piece of scenery with a hinge of book cloth pasted on with PVA. Not all scenery need be xeroxed. Very convincing accessories can be made from specialist papers. A mediaeval castle can be made from doll's house stone paper, pasted to a card foundation. Loopholes are cut from black surface paper and added to the walls. Towers are contrived by pasting stone paper on a paper former – such as the ones on which kitchen tissues are sold. Flags can be xeroxed, pasted to thin card, and then glued into the split end of barbecue skewers. The battleground itself should be not paper but thin hardboard, turned rough side up, to ensure stability. It can be covered with green cartridge paper to simulate grass, with odd tufts sticking up here and there. Rivers can be simulated by meandering strips of green and brown cellophane, ploughed fields by strips of corrugated paper. Trees can be contrived by cutting out an irregular spiky outline, rolling it into a roll with PVA adhesive pasted to it, bending back the top spikes for branches and sticking the bottom ones, outspread, on a thin, irregularly shaped cardboard base. The whole tree can then be sprayed with artist's fixative to stiffen it and foliage added by sticking crêpe paper, cut into tiny

Figure 25. Palace of Podesta – part of background scenery for a war game.

strips, to the branches. Mountains can be made up by cutting out a cardboard outline, and sticking a few lateral ribs on to the back. Thin paper is then pasted over the front and lapped over the edges to soften the outline.

A War Game from Ancient China

One of the beauties of a paper war game is that it is possible to achieve complete authenticity by utilizing prints of complete historical accuracy which can be xeroxed and worked into the game with the help of MPT. The game I am now going to describe was suggested by a treatise on warfare in old China.

A square of backing board, two feet in measurement, is laid with MPT pieces one centimetre square (0.4 in.) which could be arranged as illustrated in Fig. 13. The backing board is next covered with a sheet of good quality art drawing paper pasted on it. On the paper is drawn, first with a thin pointed pencil, and next with a Rapidograph pen or a mapping pen dipped in Indian ink, an archaic Chinese fortress. As the fortress is completely stylized in appearance it is not difficult to draw. The picture is then framed, or simply propped up from behind with a cardboard support.

The purpose of the game is for one player to hold the fortress and for the other to capture it. Defeat is conceded by taking down the flag which flies from a standard at the top of the fortress. Like all the other accessories in the game, the flag is drawn or photocopied on a sheet of paper which is then pasted to backing board and finally cut out with a piercing saw. It has a square of MPT attached to the back.

There are ten accessories in the game, five of which are weapons of attack and five of defence. Each player is given four accessories, that is he is short of one of the set, and his set need not match up with his opponents. In order to get round the problem of sharing out the accessories to each player so that neither remembers what the other has, multiple accessories are made up and they are wrapped in packs made up with shrink-a-foil (the kind of foil used to wrap sandwiches, which contracts after it has been used for wrapping). Each player takes a wrapped pack from the "defence" pack or the "attack" pack before each game begins.

At the start of the game, each player breaks his pack open. In order to play an accessory he places the accessory counter on a square of MPT set in the board. The players counter each other's ploys by placing the counter to each accessory beside it on the board.

A typical game might run as follows. The attacker begins by positioning five archers outside the fortress. The defender counters by placing a thick cloth screen on the city walls to stop the arrows. The besieger brings forward a scaling ladder to escalade the wall. The defender replies by dropping down from the wall a contrivance made from slung stones and spiked beams. The besieger attacks with a waggon full of armed assailants. The besieged replies with a "Devil Stopping Pestle", cast down from the fortress walls. Undeterred, the attacker brings up a battering ram. This is countered by a spiked carriage which blocks the breach in the wall that the battering ram has made.

By now both players have played their four pieces and the result is a stalemate. Normally, though one player would have an attack or defence piece to which the other has no counter. The other two ploys, incidentally, would have been for the attacker to try to destroy the fortress with a "Fo Lang cannon," and for the besieger to counter this by using a "Bamboo General", that is a wooden hand-gun firing stone bullets. Attacking cavalry could be dispersed by horse shackles thrown among them.

Chinese warfare of the old days is only one possible source of inspiration for a game of this sort, which could be based on virtually any period of warfare. The weapons used are all drawn, or cut from xeroxes and pasted on to card. They stick to the board by means of pieces of MPT attached to the underside. By adhering to the board they provide a continuous picture of how the game is progressing. The use of good masters for the xeroxes not merely provides authenticity, it also adds a touch of artistry to the game.

Further war games in paper have been described in Chapter 2, which covers MPT toys.

5. Toys Made from Mirror Paper

A few years ago it would have been impossible to make the toys I am going to describe without a big expenditure on mirrors, either the ready-made variety cut out or from mirror glass. One of the toys, the Polyoptic Mirror, would have been impossible to construct, because it required a commercially made tubular mirror, constructed of metal, called a speculum.

The arrival of mirror paper, Mellinex, or Mirriboard, to give it its commercial names, has changed the scene for prospective toymakers. It is now possible to construct the mirrors for the traditional toys to be described in this chapter without any tools other than a pair of scissors and a roll of double-sided sellotape. What is more, Mellinex is a lot cheaper than mirrors or mirror-glass, and, supreme advantage, it cannot shatter. So all toys made from it are completely safe to play with. Nothing is ever a complete substitute for anything else, however, and it is only fair to point out that although mirror paper reflects perfectly, the cardboard to which it is attached can warp slightly, thus altering its optical qualities somewhat. This slight distortion really affects only one of the toys I shall describe, the periscope. It is intended to be much more of a fun toy, just for looking round doors, than one which will produce an absolutely correct image. If however, you do want a more accurate periscope, for say, bird watching, all you have to do is to make up the periscope mirrors in a considerably larger size and use a square, not a round, box as the basis of the toy.

Though I mentioned the two kinds of mirror paper in the same breath a sentence or two ago, there is a basic difference between them. Mellinex is mirror paper in the roll, Mirriboard is Mellinex already bonded to thin card. Of the two, Mellinex gives the better reflection if it is well applied, but difficulties in applying it can produce the distortion I mentioned. With Mirriboard, there is no sticking down of the mirror paper to be done. It is already attached to stiff card. It can also be obtained in several colours, a selection of these usually being sold with every pack.

The Heliograph

The first toy I am going to propose to you could be, not merely a toy, but a real life-saver in moments of crisis. It is the heliograph, a message-sending mirror. The heliograph was invented back in the nineteenth-century by the British scientist, Sir Henry C. Mance. Long before Mance's time, polished shields had been used by warriors to send fairly simple messages. By using the Morse Code, however, Mance was able, by means of his swivelling mirror, to catch the light of the sun, and use it to flash a message to someone miles distant. In many ways Mance's invention has never been improved on. It is secret; an observer who was looking for a heliograph at work would fail to find it unless he was right in the path of the beam. Supposing he were looking out for a flashing signal six miles away from the heliograph transmitter. If he were only 50 yards (45 metres) out of alignment, either way of the direct bearing of the heliograph beam, he would fail to observe it. As long as the sun shone the heliograph would never break down; there was nothing to break, it was a very simple mechanism. It is impossible to jam a heliograph message and there was no possibility of anything interfering with reception.

During the late nineteenth- and early twentieth-century the British Army found the heliograph a godsend in every country where they campaigned. This did not apply to army manoeuvres in England, where the sun does not always shine, but where on the other hand a really urgent message could usually be conveyed by telephone or telegram. All over the Empire, the heliograph proved its worth. Scouting parties, cut off in the wild country of the North West Frontier in India, baffled and dismayed the armed tribesmen surrounding them by summoning up help with a message flashed back to the Khyber Pass. If no regulation heliograph were available, the message could be sent on an officer's shaving mirror. Even nowadays the heliograph has not been completely divorced from high adventure. When

Julian Nott and Colin Prescot, intrepid balloonists, were preparing to travel from Scotland to Europe by hot air balloon (a toy version of which will be described later), they packed heliographs as part of their survival kit.

A good reason to begin mirror toys with the heliograph is that it is a very simple toy to make. It is also a good introduction to the basic techniques of mirror paper work. Though you can make a heliograph from cardboard, and it will function quite well, it will not be so robust as one made from thin hardboard. Cut out an oblong of thin hardboard $7\frac{1}{4} \times 8\frac{1}{2}$ in. (184 × 215 mm.). Inside it cut out another oblong $5\frac{1}{4}$ in × $4\frac{3}{4}$ in. (133 × 121 mm). Drill the corners of this inner oblong with four holes drilled with a fine twist drill. Try to cut out the inner oblong as cleanly as possible. Once you have cut out the inner oblong, rub its edges and the edges of the frame from which it has been removed, with a piece of coarse sandpaper, folded round a straight piece of wood. When the edges of the inner oblong are well smoothed, calculate the middle of the long side of the oblong and draw a pencil line across it at right angles to the long side. Now lay the inner oblong carefully down on a sheet of Mellinex. Draw round it with a sharp pencil, then cut out the Mellinex. Look at the cut piece of Mellinex on both sides. If there are any scratches on one side, use that as the side that will be stuck to the hardboard.

I have already indicated that the most distortion-free method of applying Mellinex is to fasten it down with double-sided sellotape. To do this, tape the oblong, with up-and-down strips of the double sided tape, pull off the protecting strip, and then gently lay the Mellinex in place. Perhaps you may be unable to get double-sided sellotape, or for some reason you want to use another kind of adhesive. Thyxofix is the best adhesive for this purpose and it has already been designated as the glue to use with Mellinex. Spread the Thyxofix on both surfaces and wait till they are touch dry, then bring them together. This creates an instant bond – not necessarily an advantage if you have positioned the mirror paper wrongly over the board!

Whatever method of sticking down the Mellinex you adopt: sellotape, Thyxofix, or PVA, all of which I have tried, handle it gently as it is extremely sensitive. It will soon smear and lose its mirror-like surface if its pulled, tugged, or even rubbed too energetically. Fortunately for our first creation in Mellinex, the helio-

Toys Made from Mirror Paper

graph will work just as well whether there are a few smears of adhesive, or rub marks on the surface or not, but now is the time to learn how to handle this rather fragile, and two-sided material. It does no harm to experiment with a small piece by cementing it to a backing before you tackle the heliograph mirror. If you do have difficulties with Mellinex, you can always fall back on Mirriboard.

Once you have attached the mirror paper to the interior oblong, turn it, mirror-side down, on a pad of tissue paper, to protect the silvered surface. Take a bamboo barbecue skewer, cut off the sharp ends so that it is half an inch longer than the interior oblong, and roughen and flatten slightly one surface of it with coarse sandpaper. Now glue the skewer right along the middle line of the interior oblong that you have already marked out. Use Evo-stik to fix it, and leave a quarter of an inch protruding on either side. While you are waiting for the skewer to dry to the back of the oblong, begin work on the fittings for the mirror frame. Look round till you find a cardboard cylinder of the kind used to package rolls of paper and cut four inches (100 mm) off the end. Place it in the exact centre of the bottom edge of the frame and mark where the hollow end of the cylinder touches. Using a craft knife, cut two slots in the bottom of the frame the width of the wall of the cylinder and $\frac{3}{4}$ in. (19.05 mm) in depth. With a piercing saw cut corresponding slots in the bottom of the frame. Now push the cylinder into the bottom of the frame and stick the two together with PVA adhesive. Now attach the fittings. These are very simple. They consist of two catches to hold the ends of the barbecue skewer. Take the barrel of a used biro pen, or any other strong plastic tube, which should be double the width of the skewer. Cut half an inch from the tube. If you are using an old biro pen, cut half an inch away from the end. Saw the plastic tube down the centre with a piercing saw. Roughen the flat parts of the cut tube with coarse sandpaper. Place the mirror in the frame, mirror side down, with the ends of the barbecue skewer overlapping on the back of the frame. Coat the two bits of halved tube and the frame with Uhu glue. Glue the halved tubes in position so that they cover the protruding ends of the barbecue skewer. Once the glue has dried the mirror can revolve inside the frame, but not escape from it. Just before you glue the mirror in place, check that it really does move freely in the frame.

The next fitting to make is the holder for the cord that works the mirror. This is a square of soft wood, one inch (25 mm) square by half an inch (12.7 mm) in width. It is drilled with an eighth of an inch (3 mm) hole to take the cord, then sandpapered smooth before being stuck with Evo-stik to the back of the heliograph mirror. Now cut two round buttons out of hardboard. For each button, a $\frac{1}{2}$ in. (12.7 mm) circle of hardboard is glued to a $\frac{3}{4}$ in. (19 mm) circle. The small circles are glued to the larger ones with Evo-stik, and once they have dried, these double discs are stuck, one to the lower edge of the mirror, the other to the lower edge of the frame.

The smaller disc is on the inside, stuck to the mirror and the frame, the larger disc is on the outside. An elastic band is now looped over the two buttons so that it keeps the mirror flush with the frame. To activate the heliograph, it is now necessary to tie a length of nylon string — say 6 in. (152 mm) long — to the hole in the holder for the cord. At the other end of the string, tie a ring. You can buy plastic rings in John Galt toyshops ideal for this purpose.

The heliograph is now ready to send messages. To send efficiently, first find the compass bearing of the spot to which you intend to travel — a mountain top or wherever it may be — in relation to your base camp. There should be a conspicuous landmark at the spot you are heading towards on which you can fix your compass bearing, such as a lone tree. Tell your friends what time you expect to begin sending, and warn them to look out for your flashes at a particular time. To make sure you can locate base camp with tolerable accuracy, there is one last addition that must be made to the heliograph. Drill a $\frac{1}{2}$ in. (12.7 mm) hole through the frame, just where it meets the tube which supports it. Into this hole push and cement with PVA a cardboard tube, made just to fit. As I suggested in the first chapter, you can make this cardboard tube for yourself by wrapping stiff paper round a former, such as a $\frac{1}{4}$ in. (6.3 mm) wide length of dowel. As you wrap it, paste it with PVA and wrap the whole tube round with string, or bookbinder's tape if you have any, so as to make sure that it dries hard. Now push the tube you have made through the hole and cement it in place with PVA adhesive. By sighting through this tube you will be able to find the spot to which you intend to send messages.

Toys Made from Mirror Paper

A few final jobs require to be done. Find a stick which will just fit into the cylinder at the bottom of the frame. Sharpen one end of this to a point. Slip the cylinder over the blunt end. Complete the heliograph by painting the non-reflecting parts with black poster paint, or Humbrol enamel paint if you want the paint to be waterproof. As a help to sending messages, here is the British military heliograph code as it existed in 1911.

LETTERS				NUMBERS	
A	·—	N	—·	1	·————
B	—···	O	———	2	··———
C	—·—·	P	·——·	3	···——
D	—··	Q	——·—	4	····—
E	·	R	·—·	5	·····
F	··—·	S	···	6	—····
G	——·	T	—	7	——···
H	····	U	··—	8	———··
I	··	V	···—	9	————·
J	·———	W	·——	0	—(long)
K	—·—	X	—··—		
L	·—··	Y	—·——		
M	——	Z	——··		

Don't forget the international distress signal: SOS, but only use it in a real emergency. Heliographing is a matter of trial and error. It may take you some time to determine not merely the bearing of the spot to which you are sending a message, but also its inclination from where you stand, whether up or down.

The Designoscope

The next toy I am going to describe, the designoscope, is even easier to make than the heliograph, yet it is just as important in its practical uses. You may often have wondered how on earth professional designers manage to construct these wonderful, and very intricate patterns on fabrics, wallpaper, plastics, ceramics and all the other kinds of hand-designed products. The designoscope is the answer. It is a hinged mirror which is placed in front of the object which is going to form the basis of the design. This object could be a rosebud, a shell, a decoratively shaped nut, or anything else which offers design possibilities. The designoscope multiplies the object placed in front of it twice, four times, or even more. The picture in the mirror shows the object in different positions, but in a regular, symmetrical pattern, the kind of pattern that you do get on fabrics. To create a design, all you need to do is to choose something which is attractive, position it in the designoscope, and sketch the whole pattern as it appears. What could be simpler? Most designers make do with two hinged handbag mirrors for their designoscope, but the one which I am going to describe is much more suitable for its purpose. It is cheaper, lighter, shatter-proof, and it can be made in any size that is wanted. Decide what size you want the designoscope to be. Six and a half inches (165 mm) by four and a quarter inches (108 mm) for the two individual panels is quite a practical size. Cut two panels this size in mounting board, or other thick cardboard, using a craft knife and a metal straight edge. Check that the two panels are the same size by laying one on top of another. Now cut a hinge to fasten the two. This hinge is made of book binding cloth, and any worn and creased material you have on hand will serve, as most of the hinge will be covered.

The hinge should be a strip of cloth twice the height of the panel, plus half an inch, or in the example given above thirteen and a half inches (171 mm) long and one inch (25 mm) in width. Paste the hinge with cold water paste, and then paste the edges of the panels for $\frac{1}{2}$ in. in from the edge. Lay the edges of the panels on the centre line of the hinge, allowing a gap of a quarter of an inch between them. Paste the edges of the panels where they lie side by side on top of the cloth hinge and fold the hinge over top and bottom so that it completely covers the panels. Rub down the space between the panels with the point of a bone folder so that the cloth at the front of the panels is stuck to that at the back. Lay the pasted panels and hinge flat under a sheet of waxed paper, either proper archivist's waxed paper or the inside of a cereal packet, with a weight on top. When dry, mark a line a $\frac{1}{4}$ in. in from the centre on either side of the cloth hinge with a pencil and ruler.

Cut two oblongs of fancy paper, $\frac{3}{4}$ in. (19 mm) longer at top and bottom than the panel. These are going to be the covers for the "book" that contains the panels. The inside edge of this

Figure 26. A finished designoscope, illustrating the reflection effects on a well-known figure.

cover, the one next the hinge, must be absolutely straight, so cut it with a sharp craft knife and a straight edge. Try to position the inner line of this cover on a natural break on the pattern of the fancy paper.

Now, paste rapidly from the inside of the oblongs towards the outside, using cold water paste. Press the two pasted ends of the sheets lightly together so that they just touch, to keep them out of harm's way while you go on to paste the outsides of the panels. Do not forget your sheet of waste paper on which to paste. Lay the pasted cover, pasted side down, on top of the panel, moving it gently up to the line. Make sure the panel is in the centre of the cover. Cut off the corners of the covers with a pair of scissors, make the fold that I illustrate at the corner of the panels and fold the edge over the corners. Rub down the edges with a bone folder. Smooth down the outside of the cover with a soft duster. Lay aside the cover to dry, pressed under a sheet of waxed paper with a flat board on top and a weight on the board.

When the covers are dry, cut sheets of paper to fit inside where they lap over. In the middle of the inside of the cover there is a nasty hollow, which none of the cover paper has reached. Fill this in with a sheet of paper laid on the inside of the cover, and rubbed over with the point of a bone folder so as to show, by the crease, where the fill-in sheet will have to be cut. Remember what I said about optical distortion. If you left the inside of the cover unfilled two things would happen. The pull of the cover paper would draw the board of the cover towards it and there would not be a completely flat surface on which to position the mirror paper. Cut out two filling-in sheets and paste them in, allowing them to dry as before.

The most difficult part of making the covers is now over. All you have to do is to paste two mirrors on to the inside of each panel. With a set square and ruler mark out two Mellinex oblongs which are an eighth of an inch (3 mm) shorter all round than the inside of your panels. Cut them out with a craft knife and straight edge, making sure that the Mellinex does not peel as it is being cut. Measure up where the mirrors will go inside the panel and draw a pencil line round the oblong which they are going to fill. Carefully fill in this oblong with strips of double-sided adhesive tape laid side by side, running from top to bottom. These strips need not touch, but should lie fairly close together. Start from the top, and when the strip of double-sided tape has reached the bottom, trim it off with a craft knife, being careful not to cut into the panel.

Do not strip off the protective layer on top of the adhesive tape till you are ready to lay on them mirror paper, then pull off all the protective strips and gently lay the mirror on top, remembering that you will be unable to reposition it if it is laid down in the wrong place. Smooth down very gently with a soft cloth. The designoscope is now complete.

The flexible hinge enables you to vary the angle of the mirrors. By working out what angle the mirrors form, which you can do by placing the designoscope on a protractor, you can soon calculate how many images you will see. Set the hinges to an angle of 120°. Put a shell or some other object between the hinges. You can now see three shells in the mirrors. To find the number of images that you can see, calculate the angle in

Figure 27. Kaleidoscope with object box.

degrees. Divide 360 by the number of degrees, then subtract one from the answer. If the mirrors are at an angle of 45°, divide 360 by 45. The answer is 8. Now take away one and 7 is left.

The Kaleidoscope

There can be no question as to which toy made from mirrors has had the greatest success. The kaleidoscope is easily the favourite mirror toy of all time. Within three months of its invention by the great Scottish scientist, Sir David Brewster, 200,000 kaleidoscopes were sold in London and Paris. One reason why the kaleidoscope has always been so popular with children is that it shows a symmetrical design which changes every time you shake the toy. It is also possible to make up several different *object boxes* so that the items that make up the coloured design in the toy can be changed.

In essence the kaleidoscope is a three-sided box, whose inside faces are lined with mirrors. There is no bottom to the box, but there is a top, pierced with an eye hole. The bottom of the kaleidoscope is pushed into an *object box*, a triangular box with a rim at the top, which just fits to the bottom of the kaleidoscope. Inside this *object box* are a collection of small, and brightly coloured objects. The triple mirrors of the kaleidoscope reflect these objects in a six-sided, symmetrical picture. A shake of the hand alters the whole picture; furthermore, by removing one object box from the bottom and substituting another, an entirely different collection of coloured objects can be brought into view.

The kaleidoscope is made up on much the same principles as the designoscope. Start by cutting out the panels for the mirrors. They are made of backing board or other thick cardboard and are 9 × 3 in. (228 × 76 mm) long and broad. Cut the panels as evenly as you can, by using a sharp craft knife and straight edge, and place them on top of one another just to satisfy yourself that they are really all the same size. Lay the panels on a piece of Mellinex, mark round them with a sharp pencil, and cut out the marked out shapes. Lay them aside for the moment.

Now cut an oblong of book binding cloth which is to act as a universal hinge that goes right round all three panels. This oblong should be 13 × 9 in. (330 × 228 mm). It need not be the best bookcloth – in fact it can be badly creased or worn as it will all be covered anyhow. Place the panels on the uncoloured inside of the book cloth, which is the more absorbent of the two. Draw a straight line across the book cloth, $\frac{1}{4}$ in. from the right-hand edge of the long side. Lay one panel on this line and run round it with a pencil to mark its place. Measure $\frac{1}{4}$ in. in from the left-hand side of the panel, and draw a straight line. Lay the second panel up against that, mark it out as before. Go on till you have marked the places for the three panels. You are now left with an extra piece of cloth without a panel on it, on the left. Cut off the top and bottom corners of this oblong, so that it will serve as a flap to wrap round the remaining pieces of cloth which have been stuck to the back of the panels.

Take some PVA adhesive, and paste both the places where the panels are to sit, and one side of each panel. Position the panels on the marked spots, rub down the cloth on to the pasted side of the panels with a bone folder. Leave the panels, now stuck to the cloth, under a heavy weight to dry.

Only now should you add the Mellinex mirrors to the panels. If you did it before, then some paste would be sure to adhere to the mirror paper, smearing it and spoiling the reflection. Attach the mirrors to the panels with double-sided sellotape.

The whole kaleidoscope box can now be put together. Paste the loose flap, and paste the cloth covered back of the panel to which it will be attached. Bring them together, rubbing down the

Toys Made from Mirror Paper 77

cloth flap with a bone folder. Twist elastic bands round the kaleidoscope body till the flap has dried in place, which will not take long.

Now cut a triangle of mounting board, just the size to fit over the top of the box. Use a protractor to make sure that each corner of the triangle forms an angle of 60°. Using a $\frac{1}{4}$ in. Xacto knife, punch a hole in the centre of the triangle, then paint one side of it with black poster paint. Once the paint on the triangle is dry dab the edges of the triangle with PVA adhesive and cement them to the top of the kaleidoscope. This top is now the eyepiece, through which the mirror image can be viewed.

Now make up the object box out of thin perspex sheet. Often a food package box can be adapted for this purpose, such as the perspex boxes used for some merchandizing. Cut three half-inch strips of perspex, longer than the sides of the kaleidoscope box.

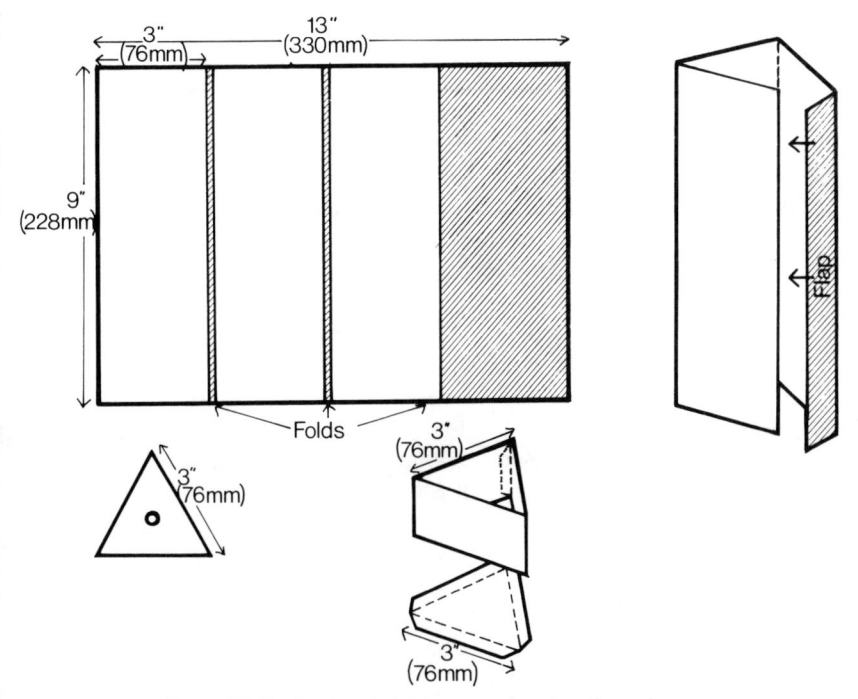

Figure 28. Design for a kaleidoscope, showing dimensions.

Using the box as a pattern, trim the strips (using a piercing saw) till they just join on the outside of the kaleidoscope. Keeping them on the kaleidoscope as a former, glue them together with Polystyrene cement (the kind used for sticking plastic models together). Keep them in place with an elastic band till they have cemented together. You now have a triangle of perspex strips. Use this as a template to mark out the base of the box from sheet perspex. The base can be of rather thicker perspex. Cement the sides of the object box on to the base. Now cut a triangle of thin perspex which will just fit inside the box. Try this for size but do not cement it in yet, instead put it to one side. In order to produce the best optical image, the sides of the perspex should be smoothed down with a file or sandpaper, once they have been cut. You may also decide to polish the perspex pieces, using perspex polish, once they have been completed. If you are going to have interchangeable boxes for the kaleidoscope, make up more than one. Three is a good number to construct. A few bright small objects must be placed in each box, so that when jumbled, they will produce a pattern. Here are just some of the kind of objects you may want to include: pieces of tinsel, spangles, small tumbled stones, coloured plastic beads and small geometrical shapes of plastic, silver charms from Christmas puddings, initials and shapes (such as snowflake patterns) cut from coloured Mirriboard, antique beads, such as a single jet bead or a seed pearl. Attractive object box collections can be made from small natural objects, such as tiny fronds of coloured seaweeds, small brightly coloured shells and small pieces of broken iridescent shell, such as Abalone (all of which can be got from Friedlein and Co, London) A few grains of coloured sand can also be included.

As each object box is filled, cement in the top before the small objects get a chance to scatter. You can do this quite easily by having some item in each box that is $\frac{1}{4}$ in. long. Prop this up on one end and lower the top of the box gently on to it. Then run plastic cement round the edges of the join. The "prop" could be an initial cut from coloured plastic. Once it starts getting shaken about it will soon fall flat. As each object box is completed, try it out.

All that now needs to be done is to cover the outside of the kaleidoscope with fancy paper. Cut an oblong of patterned paper so broad that it just overlaps the three sides of the box. The top of

Toys Made from Mirror Paper

the oblong is cut into three triangles, which will meet and overlap over the eye-hole. These triangles are pasted so that they cover the eyepiece, then the eyepiece is cut through again with a punch by placing the kaleidoscope on top of a wooden batten, held in the vice over which the lid is placed. Be careful not to rub the Mellinex with this batten. The paper cover can be pasted on either with cold water paste or PVA adhesive. As the kaleidoscope will have to stand a good deal of handling, give it a protective coating. Self-adhesive plastic film, the kind used for covering books, will do well for this, while a coating of matt acrylic varnish will also give some protection.

The Periscope

There is no need for me to repeat the warning I gave earlier as we approach our next toy. The smaller the size of the *Periscope*, the greater will be the optical distortion. Nonetheless, as small periscopes are very easily made, and because they will always give *some* kind of an image (such as showing whether anyone is waiting round the corner to hit you on the head with a pillow), it is worth while beginning with a small sized version of this toy, and then making a larger one if it is required.

The basis for the small periscope is a cardboard tube, of the kind used to roll paper round. Select the largest cardboard tube you can find and trim its edges, which are probably ragged. You can do this very neatly by folding a piece of paper round the tube so that the ends overlap, marking the line thus described and cutting it through carefully with a craft knife. Now measure the circle *inside* the cardboard tube with a pair of dividers. This will give you the size of the periscope mirrors.

Using a pair of compasses, draw out a circle of this size on thick paper. Mark out four circles this size. Paste two of them on to mounting board. These are the patterns for the backs of the periscope mirrors. Cut them out with a piercing saw from the mounting board as soon as they are dry. The other two paper discs are going to be used as templates for cutting out the apertures of the periscope. These apertures will be at top and bottom of the tube, but they will be on different sides. Draw lines down each face of the tube so that they exactly divide it. Stick one paper circle at one end of the tube, a quarter of an inch down, and the other at the other end but on the opposite side.

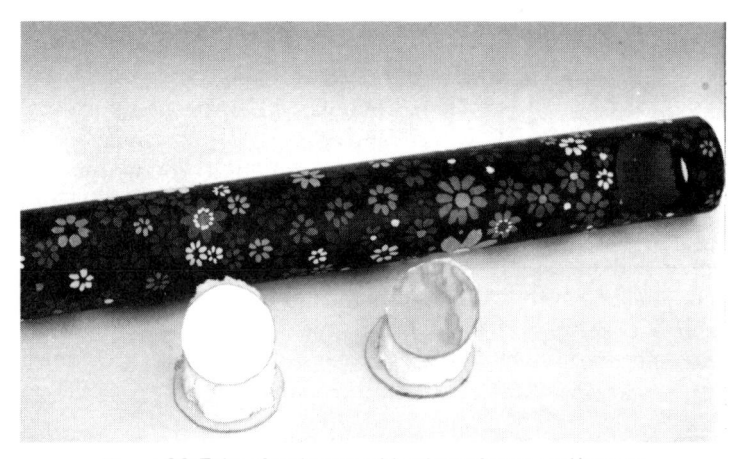

Figure 29. Tube of periscope with mirrors for top and bottom.

Now lay the two circles cut from mounting board on Mellinex, and pencil them round. Cut out the Mellinex with embroidery scissors. Fasten the mirrors to the roundels using double-sided sellotape. Now cut out the circular apertures at top and bottom of the periscope, using a sharp pointed craft tool such as a small sized Xacto knife.

Get some polystyrene and cut out a circular cork that will just push into the tube. This should be the length of your mirror's diameter. Cut two mounting board roundels the exact size of the outside of the tube, and stick the cork to one of them, using wood glue such as Evo-stik. Now mark a line half an inch up from the cardboard roundel on the polystyrene cork and cut the remaining part of the cork away at an angle of 90°. Paste the mirrors to the corks with PVA adhesive. Once they are dry, try them out. Push one in at one end of the periscope, and the other at the opposite end. A little twisting will bring them into alignment, when you ought to get a fair image, in the bottom mirror, of what the top one can "see".

Finish the periscope by gluing the corks into the ends of the tube with PVA and by covering the whole of the periscope with brightly patterned paper. The cardboard roundels topping the corks can be finished off with the brightly coloured paper stickers or transfers that can be bought in paper shops.

With the principles of the small periscope in mind, you can go

Toys Made from Mirror Paper 81

on to make a very much larger one, say from one of those circular boxes in which bottles of whisky or sherry are sometimes packed. This can be camouflaged with grey paper and a few twigs and will prove invaluable for bird watching.

The Polyoptic Mirror
The next toy that I am going to describe, the polyoptic mirror, has not been made for at least a hundred years. The polyoptic mirror was a toy which consisted of two parts, one a distorted picture, laid flat on the table. This picture was so distorted as to be quite unrecognizable. It was either painted or printed. The other part of the toy consisted of a "speculum", a word which in Latin means just "mirror". The speculum was a tube of bright metal, or a cylinder of glass mirrored inside with mercury. When the speculum was placed on a circle printed at the bottom of the grotesque drawing sheet, lo and behold, the distorted face turned into that of a beautiful lady or a handsome young officer. The different segments of the distorted picture had been condensed by the tubular reflection and returned to the shape of the original model.

Often these polyoptic mirrors had not been toys, but serious ways of projecting a picture of someone whose portrait it would have been treasonable to carry about. Jacobites carried distorted pictures of the Old Pretender and used a speculum to display his recognizable portrait to a few fellow sympathizers.

A few years ago it would have been virtually impossible for the amateur toymaker to construct this polyoptic mirror. Now nothing is easier. All you need is a tube of cardboard covered with a sheet of Mellinex fixed to the tube with double-sided sellotape.

This is placed on top of a sheet of paper, containing a distorted drawing. The drawing then resumes its natural proportions in the mirror. Professor Pepper, of the Old Regent St. Polytechnic of London, a famous illusionist and creator of "Pepper's Ghost," described in the next chapter, has explained how you go about creating the distorted pictures which the mirror brings back to normal proportions. All that you need to do is to make a cardboard cylinder of the same size as your mirror. It has two windows in it, one large, one rather smaller behind it on the opposite side of the cylinder. The cardboard cylinder is laid

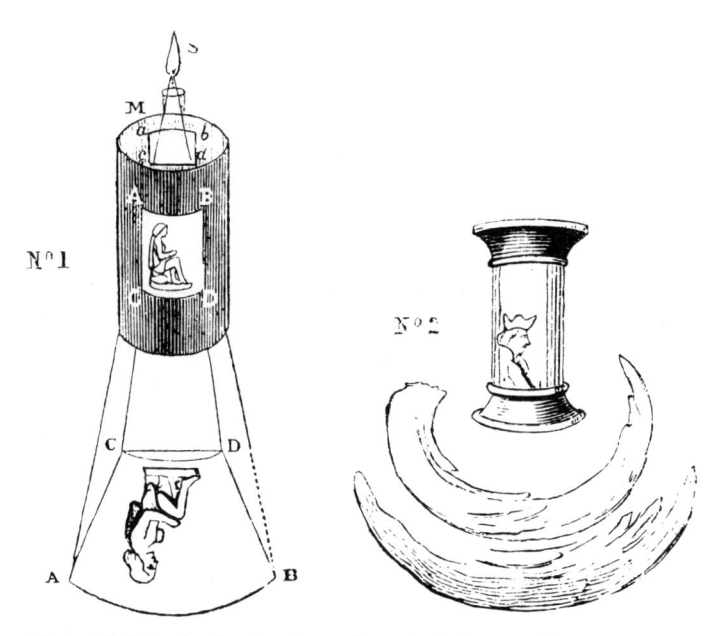

Figure 30. Old print showing Pepper's method of drawing polyoptic mirror pictures.

on the table on a sheet of white paper. A small lamp is placed so that its rays shine through the small window, out through the larger one, and onto the paper. Pepper himself used a candle, but a small hand lamp would do, provided its rays were directed right at the small window. A drawing was then slipped into the cylinder so that it formed an inset for the larger window. Pepper perforated the lines of this drawing by pricking them through with a pin. His drawing was made on paper. Yours could be made on anything transparent, such as acetate, drawn on with ink markers. In any case the light projects a distorted picture on to the paper, which is then sketched in in outline. You can then colour the drawing, and place it under the speculum, when it will resume its life-like proportions. If you are very lucky, you may even be able to find in an antique shop old polyoptic pictures, such as those published by Walter Frère in Paris about 1850.

Distorting Mirrors
Having discovered for yourself, by making up the polyoptic mirror, that odd shaped mirrors produce odd reflections, it is a

Toys Made from Mirror Paper

small step to creating mirrors that deliberately distort. It is easier to make distorting mirrors in Mellinex than in any other material, because there is always a certain amount of optical distortion with sheet Melline. You can, with very little trouble, create a "Hall of Mirrors" which will give amusingly distorted images of yours and your friends' faces. The cardboard cylinders used to package some liquor bottles make ideal backings for concave and convex mirrors, placed horizontally and vertically. Other, and much simpler ideas, are worth trying. Just a few spots of paste left on a flat mirror underneath the Mellinex before it is rubbed down will make your face look as though it had spots on it. A flat square mirror with one of the corners bending gradually inwards produces an odd reflection. An ordinary piece of Mirriboard or Mellinex covered cardboard framed as a hall mirror will usually produce alarm and consternation in visitors if it has a fearsome bug painted on it.

If you want to, you can combine several different distorting mirrors on a turntable, which can be placed on a tall piece of furniture, such as the shelf of a room divider and then turned round slowly, so that visitors can see their faces in each of the mirrors in turn.

It is very easy to make up such a turntable. First cut out a circle of plywood three feet across. Sand this down, then prime it and finally paint it a matt black. Cut another circle of the same size and finish it in the same way. Now get a wooden or plastic reel, of the kind used to package thread. Glue this in the bottom of one of the circles. Now find a short length of wooden dowel which will just fit into the hole in the reel. Glue this in the exact centre of the other circle. Now fit the dowel into the reel so that the top circle can be spun round slowly. The top circle carries all the mirrors which will have to be made reasonably small, say nine inches high. You can, if you like, put a circular fascia round and above the mirrors carrying some such lettering as: "See yourselves as others see you", or "Mirrors cannot lie".

The Praxinoscope

The next mirror toy which I am going to describe — the Praxinoscope — is much easier to make in Mellinex than in ordinary mirror glass. Like the polyoptic mirror, the praxinoscope too is a tubular mirror. Instead of being placed on a sheet of paper, however, it is mounted on a stand inside a circular well. Round the sides of the well are a series of movement pictures, arranged in sequence. A typical series might show a juggler throwing up several coloured balls into the air, then catching them again. As the well revolves round the tubular mirror, the figures cease to appear still. They jump into life and appear to move. Like another toy that is described in this book, the thaumatrope, the praxinoscope depends on what is called "continuity of vision". Our eye bridges over the gaps between the jerky motions that the figures really describe in the mirror. Instead, we see them move in a lifelike motion.

Because the true-to-life action of the toy depends very much on its rapid and easy spinning motion, it is as well to make the moving part of the mechanism first. The turning motion of the praxinoscope is imparted by a mechanism very like the one I described for the turntable with the distorting mirrors. It is made up by taking two wooden or plastic bobbins and a length of round wooden dowel, sufficiently long to go right through the central hole of both bobbins. Half the length of dowel is glued into one wooden bobbin. The bobbin in turn is glued to the exact centre of a stout wooden base, a wood block say 10 × 10 inches square and 2 inches thick. This base must be sandpapered and varnished with polyurethane varnish. The loose bobbin can now be placed on top of the dowel. The end of the dowel should not protrude above it, and the bobbin should be able to spin freely, with a flick of the finger. It will not spin properly unless the stand is exactly level and the bottom bobbin and length of dowel are glued to it so that they are exactly upright.

Now for the well. This can often be obtained, ready made, in the shape of a hat box, plastic ice cream tub, or any other circular container. Find the exact centre of the bottom of the box on the underside, and mark it.

Now make up the mirror, which is the easiest feature of the toy to make. The mirror should be the same height as the depth of the well, and about one third of the diameter of the whole well. Plastic bottles, cut down to size, plastic tubes for holding pills and the stout cardboard cores of reels of electric flex (cord) all spring to mind as likely ready-made objects which can be pressed into use as a mirror support with virtually no trouble. Even if you cannot find a cylinder just the size you want, it re-

Toys Made from Mirror Paper

quires little labour to build up a cardboard cylinder by wrapping thin card round a circular former, such as a paint spray can, and gluing it with PVA as you build up the thicknesses. The card is pulled tight as it is wound round, then held in place by twisted elastic rubber bands. In a few moments it will have dried. Brush the completed card cylinder with more PVA adhesive and it makes it more rigid, then pare away the join mark, where the meeting of the cardboard strips show, with a sharp craft knife. Trim the ends. Now all you have to do is to prepare a circular top for the central mirror from card, and finish this top off by sticking a coloured paper rosette, of the kind you can buy in any paper shop, on top of it. Now, using double-sided sellotape, apply Mellinex to the drum of the central mirror.

Set it aside and finish the praxinoscope well. Spray the interior of the well with matt white plastic paint, and decorate the outside of the well with a strip of fancy paper. Mark the exact centre of the inside of the well, and with a compass, draw round it a circle the exact size of the base of the central mirror. Dab some PVA to the bottom of the mirror base, being careful not to get any adhesive on the mirror paper and stick it down. The well is now ready for a test spin on top of the base. Using a compass, draw a circle the exact size of the bobbin on the underside of the well, using the already marked centre position. Cement the bobbin in place with Uhu or other impact cement. When the bobbin has dried, place the well, resting on its bobbin, on top of the protruding dowel spindle. Spin it round with your finger to make sure it is revolving easily.

In order to spin the praxinoscope sufficiently fast to produce the "continuity of vision" illusion, that makes you think you can really see the figures in the central mirror moving, all you have to do is to tie a long line of thin, strong, thread, such as nylon string, round the top bobbin. Twist the top bobbin. Twist the bobbin round till all the thread has been wound round it. Then give the thread a sharp pull and keep pulling till all the thread has unwound. The praxinoscope will spin round in rapid motion and the figures in the band (which we will make up in a few moments) will be reflected in the central mirror in lively motion (if a little distorted because of the curve of the mirror).

Years ago, in Victorian times when the praxinoscope was invented, the bands of figures which fitted inside the well must have been the most difficult part of the toy to make. They must have been so difficult to construct that they were probably never made by amateurs, but simply bought (one enterprising American haberdasher of 1836 even produced special hat boxes lined with figure bands for a toy that was closely related to the praxinoscope, the Zoetrope[1]).

Nowadays, making a praxinoscope strip is a much easier affair. All you need is a little patience, a few pennies, the use of a xerox machine, and a good master drawing. Of course there is nothing to stop you creating your master drawing for yourself, drawing a figure of a juggler, a clown, a seal, an athlete or acrobat, or any other suitable figure for a strip. But if you can find a good figure in a book or old magazine this will give you a head start.

Begin by working out how many times the figure can be repeated on the strip you are going to make up for the inside of the well. The strip should be the height of the well, it should be of good art paper, and it should be of just the length to go right round the inside of the well and overlap slightly. There should be preferably about twelve appearances of the figure on the strip, so do not choose any figure that will take up too much room. Mark twelve equal sections on your strip. Now make xeroxes of the figure you have chosen. Alternatively, just copy them twelve times on to your strip by tracing them, afterwards going over the lines in Indian ink. If you xerox the figure either cut out the whole outline of the figure with embroidery scissors, or (much more simply) cut out a square of paper the exact height of the band with the figure of the juggler or seal in the middle.

Your twelve-times repeated figure has now been pasted down on the band. If you are using either of the two figures I have given as illustrations, all you have to do now is to add a ball that the seal has thrown up with its nose. Get some coloured circular stickers the right size for a circus ball, and stick one just above the seal's nose in its "first position". Go on round all the other eleven, making the ball rise higher, then fall back, so that the last ball you stick down has almost landed on the seal's nose again. If you are using the juggler, do the same thing, but give him four coloured balls (smaller than the seal's) which he throws

---

[1] See *Making Scientific Toys*.

Toys Made from Mirror Paper

into the air and then catches in his hands again. When the praxinoscope is spun round the figures will flicker into movement.

This chapter can conclude with a simply made toy which can be quite disconcerting. Make up a thaumatrope in the way I have described in Chapter 9. On one side stick down a fearsome looking bug, about life size, which you have cut from a magazine. Cover the whole of the other side with Mellinex. When you spin the thaumatrope the insect will appear to be sitting on your nose.

6. Paper Entertainments

Anyone who has read this chapter heading may feel inclined to say: "Surely paper entertainments must be confined to the toy theatre." I am going to talk about the toy theatre in the next chapter, and also the shadow play, but what I would like to emphasize right at the outset is that there are many ways of entertaining a crowd, a few friends, or even one child that are never put in to practice nowadays. The topics I am going to write about in this chapter are the traditional forms of paper amusement which have been allowed to die out.

The Diorama
Take the Diorama for example. If you had been a well-behaved American child in the year 1868 your father might have bought you a diorama, made by that enterprising American toymaker, Milton Bradley. Bradley's Diorama was called: "The Historoscope – Panorama and History of America from Columbus to the Civil War." It was a box which contained two spindles on which a roll of paper was wound. As you turned one spindle it wound paper off the other. One side of the box was made up to look like the proscenium of a toy theatre. The owner of the diorama turned a handle in the box and the paper roll unwound behind the proscenium. One exciting picture after another appeared on "the stage," first Columbus, of course, then the Pilgrim Fathers in the *Mayflower*, and so on. As long as the roll kept unwinding the audience was enthralled. Everybody was keen to see what was going to come next.

The toy was a child's version of an adult amusement. In the London of 1854 you could visit the *Diorama of the Ganges* (in India, then a British possession) in "a very beautiful and much

Paper Entertainments

admired lounge, called the Portland Gallery, situated at No 316. Regent St (Langham Place) opposite the Polytechnic Institution. Pianist, Herr Adolph, Lecturer Mr. S. Walsh, machinery by Mr. Cooper, figures and animals painted by Mr. Buss; the diorama exquisitely painted by Mr. T.C. Dibdin, from the admirable sketches by James Ferguson, Esq., made during a long residence in India. Doors open at half-past two and half-past seven P.M. Admission one shilling, reserved seats two and sixpence."

Like the child's toy, the grown-up amusement was meant to be educative as well as instructive. You would see some of the wonderful scenery for which India is famous, its temples and jungles, cities and deserts. There would be pictures of the peoples and animals of India rolling past to the accompaniment of a commentary and some appropriate music which would perhaps recall the rhythms of Indian music.

Children too poor to buy their own dioramas made them for themselves or had them made by an adult. At the beginning of this century Robert Tressall wrote a book called *The Ragged Trousered Philanthropists,* in which one of the characters, a man called Bert White, brings to a Christmas Party a toy he has made. He calls it his "Pandoramer," which was, as he explained, "a show, like what they have at the Hippodrome" (a London music hall). Bert supplied his own orchestra, in the shape of a mouth organ.

"The 'Pandoramer', says Tressall, "consisted of a stage front made of painted cardboard and fixed on the front of a wooden box about three-feet long by two-feet six-inches high and about one-foot deep. The 'show' consisted of a lot of pictures cut out of illustrated weekly papers and pasted together, end to end, so as to form a long strip, or ribbon. Bert had painted all the pictures with water colours.

Just behind the wings of the stage front, at each end of the box, was an upright roller on which the long strip of pictures was rolled. The upper ends of the rollers came through the top of the box and had handles attached to them. When the handles were turned the pictures passed across the stage, unrolling from one roller and rolling on to the other, and they were illuminated by the light of three candles placed behind."

Whenever he got to a highlight in his show, Bert stopped turning the rollers, seized his mouth organ, and played a tune that everyone recognized, so that the audience could join in.

There is nothing easier than to build a diorama on Bert White lines — but not necessarily Bert White size. To start with, anyhow, it is much better to construct a miniature diorama, one whose unrolling strip of paper will take less filling up to create the entertainment, and one which can be planned to the size of a small, ready-made roll of tape, such as the 'machine rolls' that are used in cash registers. Nor is there any need at this first attempt for the diorama to be lit up from behind. Instead take a leaf out of Milton Bradley's book and construct a diorama with a proscenium modelled on a real theatre. The proscenium need not occupy the whole of the front of the diorama, it is merely the window behind which the unrolling strip will appear. Creating the proscenium is a very simple affair. Find some illustration of an old theatre proscenium front, which will not be hard to find, as every book about the history of the theatre will have several. Photostat this illustration of a proscenium, preferably on one of the photostat machines which claim to be able to copy photographs as clearly as the original. Paste the whole of your photostat on thin card-like mounting board.

Now have a look at the machine roll you are going to use for the diorama roll. Adapt the proscenium to it by cutting away a big enough stage opening to allow most of the width of the roll to show, leaving a margin at top and bottom that does not show. If you are lucky enough to have found a theatre just the size you want for your roll, well and good. Cut a square or oblong opening in the proscenium through which you will be able to see the show being rolled past. If the theatre you have is slightly too big for the roll you have, leave a curtain hanging part of the way down towards the stage. Even if there is no curtain on your original illustration you can paint one in and then cut the bottom of the curtain to the size you want. You can even add a curtain of thin card stuck behind the proscenium opening. I found an illustration of a Redington toy theatre, made in 1860, which was exactly the size I wanted. If you cannot find a suitable illustration, try drawing a theatre proscenium with a Rapidograph pen.

Now you have the opening through which the audience will be able to see your show. You now need the complete stage front, but before you make this up, first construct the machinery which will enable you to turn the rollers. The machinery for the

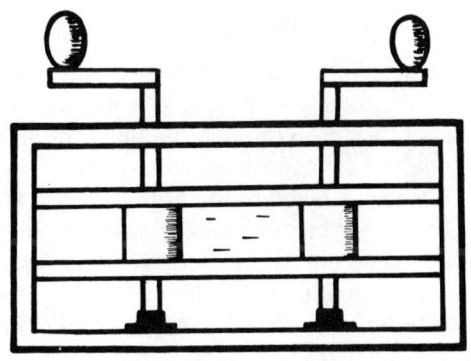

Figure 31. Back view of diorama with proscenium removed.

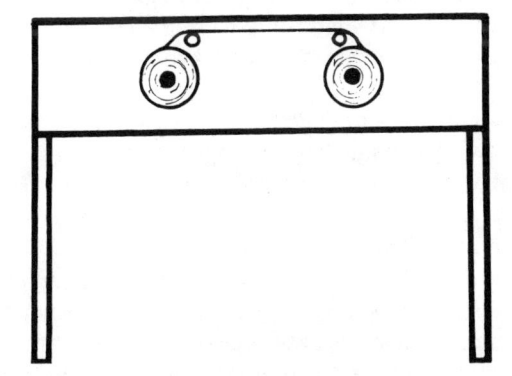

Figure 32. Middle section view of diorama from on top to show doors hinged back.

winders and rollers which I illustrate is, as you can see for your self, a very simple constructional job. It is an oblong of two-inch (50 mm) wood batten, with two interior crossbars between which rest the wooden rollers. Two holes are drilled through the frame to take the rollers, which simply drop through the hole in the middle of the centre core of the machine roll reel. Before the roller is pushed into the machine roll core, something is put inside the roll so that it will wedge in place, such as a thin strip of card. As you only get one core with each machine roll, you will have to make up a spare core by winding card round a former and pasting it in place with PVA. To this core the loose end of the roll will be attached with double-sided sellotape when you start the show. The rollers are kept revolving in a completely vertical position because they drop through the holes in the top, of the frame and the first and second crossbars, and at the bottom they rest in nylon bushes screwed to the bottom of the frame. I just happened to have these bushes when I began making this toy, as they came from some dismantled folding doors. Two pieces of plastic tube cemented to pieces of flat plastic would have done instead. I left the rollers revolving in the bushes and allowed gravity to keep them in place. I could have drilled holes through the bushes and pushed a wood screw, held by a washer, into the bottom of each roller.

Two wooden spindles, whose ends have been drilled, are kept in place by four wooden pegs glued into the crossbars to top and bottom of them. Their function is to keep the paper of the roll pressed hard against the proscenium window. Two folding doors are hinged to the back of the frame. When the diorama is stored away they are closed and hooked together with a hook and eye catch. While the show is going on they are unhooked and opened out. They rest on the top of the table where the diorama is being operated and give stability.

The more solidly the framework is put together, and the greater care given to the placing of the pieces so that they are all at right angles or really parallel to one another, the better the diorama will perform. Looks do not matter because the whole of the frame will be covered by a front, with the proscenium attached to it.

How to fill in the front of the diorama around the proscenium is a problem that can be tackled in several ways. One way is to make several photostats of the theatre illustration and cut strips from the sides of each, showing side boxes. These strips can be pasted on either side of the proscenium, giving the impression of the interior of an old theatre.

I have said nothing so far about the rollers and the handles that turn them. The rollers are made from round dowel, drilled at one end, and with a bolt glued in. The handles are made up from pieces of scrap wood to which are attached turned wooden knobs screwed on to one end. The other end of the handle joining section is fastened with a nut on to the bolt protruding from the roller end.

Paper Entertainments

The diorama is completed by making an oblong of backing board which is the exact size of the frame and which is screwed to the frame with small wood screws. The proscenium opening is of course aligned so that it is placed right in front of the part of the strip unwound between the two rollers.

It is good policy to make sure that proscenium and rolling strip are properly aligned and also to find out what parts of the strip will be covered with pictures before the show can begin. Do this by getting a friend to help you turn the rollers while you hold the points of two pencils pressing lightly against the strip at the top and bottom of the proscenium opening. Apply only the lightest of pressure to the turning roll of paper, pressing against the spindle, or else you will tear it.

Now comes the moment when you have to make up your roll, and before you do this you must have a complete idea of what you want to create. Diorama rolls should be scenic, they should also be exciting. Fairly uneventful scenes should alternate with the more exciting ones so that the viewer's interest is secured and held to the final scene. Here are just a few ideas for dioramas: a ballon race across the Alps during a storm, a voyage down the Amazon on a *jandaga* or sailing raft, or a trip across the Prairies of the Old West.

Begin by planning out what types of scenes and incidents there will be on the roll and roughly how much space they will occupy. Take the roll and spread out as much of it as you can on a big flat surface. Mark it off into sections and begin work, preferably with the help of a few friends, all of whom make a section.

I suggest you use different kinds of artwork so as to fill in the roll. Like the *Diorama of the Ganges*, parts of the roll can be "exquisitely painted" by yourself. Keep your painting to the easier stretches of the trip to depict, say, the rolling fields of golden corn in Illinois, with blue skies above, painted in the impressionistic manner of the artist Renoir. The more blurred the painting looks, the more realistic it will appear, because we will assume we are speeding across the Prairie in a passenger car of one of the old railroads, and scenery *does* look blurred when a locomotive begins to pick up speed.

From time to time something a little more detailed will appear on this rolling landscape. It could be a farmhouse with its windmill or a stationary locomotive and its line of cars. Draw these with a Rapidograph pen.

When you have to depict anything the least bit elaborate, such as a squadron of US cavalry, a herd of buffalo, or mounted Pawnees on the warpath, use the Letraset figures which can be bought in small albums. These figures seem to be absolutely designed for a small diorama such as this. Cut out some of the scenery from the album too, and paste it in so that you can use pieces of the printed album to indicate stations, forts and ranches.

If you cannot find just the picture that you want, photostat an illustration from an old book. Any picture of an old station can be made to serve your turn — western urban architecture was usually very like that back east — if you set up a noticeboard near the station with the legend: "Welcome to Prairie City", just to show the viewers where they are. A dip into a few old books such as George Catlin's illustrated accounts of his travels will fascinate you, as well as providing illustrations of real portraits of Indians that can be photostated.

Be as ingenious as you like. If you want to depict a prairie fire, brush the roll with paste and stick down leaping tongues of flame cut from red and yellow metallic foil paper.

There is no reason why you should not, from time to time introduce stage properties between you and the viewers. You could, for example, have a cut-out figure of an Indian, mounted in the way I have described under military modelling, and drop it down suddenly from the top of the proscenium on the end of a wire, at the same time firing off some caps to indicate gunfire. Another property which can be introduced in a toy of this sort is a railroad car — preferably the caboose of the train, which can be dropped in from the top from time to time to show that you are just catching up with the end of the train. "Props" of this sort are not difficult to make from illustrations, often found in old books, and mounted in the same way as military miniatures, or the stage characters for the toy theatre that I am going to describe in the next chapter.

An interesting variant of the Victorian style diorama is a diorama where only the foreground moves and the back scenery remains static. Figures and objects appear moving across a background. The background can be seen because the figures are mounted on a roll of transparent acrylic roll which slowly unwinds. More and more figures appear in turn. They are cut from rather thin paper, such as the paper used on photostat machines, and they are pasted to the acrylic roll.

Apart from the scenic background, which like the figures themselves, is photostated, mounted on card and screwed to the front of the framework, underneath the proscenium, the construction of the moving diorama offers few changes from the construction of the traditional Victorian diorama. One further change is that it is possible to do away with the spindles pressing the acrylic roll against the proscenium opening, because the background keeps the acrylic pressed close to the proscenium opening. Another change is that for paper machine rolls, rolls of acrylic are substituted. It is not practical for the amateur toy-maker to paint or draw on acrylic, so instead, photostated figures are pasted to the roll with PVA adhesive.

I found the raw material for my moving diorama in a children's book published many years ago. This featured, among other illustrations a view of the Houses of Parliament from the South Bank. In the foreground of this picture a tug with several barges was chugging up river I thought that it would be splendid if there could be a continuous stream of river traffic passing up past the Houses of Parliament in the picture so I set about constructing a diorama where this would happen. First I xeroxed the picture several times. Next, with the embroidery scissors, I cut one of the photostat copies of the picture in half, just at the waterline of the Thames. Then I pasted this half sheet on to a sheet of backing board, which was about an inch larger in size all round about than the whole picture. The space below the waterline was now blank. I cut to size and pasted on to this a strip of green cellophane to suggest water. Green metallic foil-covered paper would have done as well. The cellophane covered all the space which the river had covered in the illustration.

Now I had to deal with the foreground, the part below the river. This was extremely intricate and I cut it out with embroidery scissors, pasted it on a sheet of clear acrylic, and framed it with a hollow oblong of backing board. On reflection perhaps I would have done better to mount the foreground on cardboard and cut it out with a piercing saw, but as it stood, the foreground made an ideal proscenium. All I needed to do now was to construct the roll, which would unroll between the proscenium and the background I had just made, which would both be screwed to the frame with the same screws, with short pieces of backing board as spacing pieces in between.

I now cut a length of acrylic which was slightly wider than the depth of the picture and positioned it on the rolls of the frame I had constructed to hold it. At suitable positions on the roll I pasted down tugs, shipping, barges, a pleasure boat and so forth; all of these had been photostated and then cut out with embroidery scissors. Finally I cut a mat of mounting board of the kind used to frame pictures, and then positioned a wooden picture frame over the whole diorama by pushing the edges of the diorama into the recess of the frame and gluing them there with impact adhesive.

This kind of toy admits to many modifications. If you want to, you can remove the visible handles and feature a side drive, worked by a Mecanno bevel gear (No. 30c) driven by a pulley (No. 23) connected by a short axle. The pulley is outside the frame and is connected with the bevel gear by an axle which runs through a hole in the frame. The roller is drilled to admit a long Mecanno axle being glued into it. The large bevel gear is fitted to its top.

The picture begins to move when the left or right hand roller is fully wound up by hand. The rollers are then wound by pulling a continuous cord passed through the pulley. The picture now unrolls. One benefit of this arrangement is that quite a small child can work the mechanism, should need be, from some distance away. So the moving diorama with pulley attachment would provide an ideal bedtime toy which could be worked by its owner from inside his or her cot. Afterwards, of course, the cord is removed.

Many moving dioramas can be made which have much simpler arrangements than the one I have suggested. Usually there is no need to cut the background up as I did here. Anything that appears on it that is not wanted can be painted out with a mixture of Chinese white and Indian ink. Some very simple moving dioramas can still be effective – what about a diorama of the Taxis of the Marne for example? Here all you would need would be a photostat of a French street and enough scale pictures of old taxis to fill the roll.

The figures on moving dioramas need not be cut from photostats. They could be Letraset figures stuck down, then sprayed with fixative. Anyone who wanted to make a diorama of a bridge, or a city street, with traffic moving across it would simply buy one of those sheets of multiple cars. Sheets of multiple human figures are also ideal for constructing dioramas of streets, while the albums of adventure figures which I have already referred to are also very handy. You could make an historical diorama of figures moving across some scenic background like the great American desert, and have first primitive man, then the Indians, then the pioneers and finally the people of today moving across it.

It is a simple matter to motorize a diorama by adding an electric motor, battery, and an on and off switch.

The Peepshow and Pepper's Ghost

Many toys are small-scale versions of large-scale amusements. The Peepshow is an example. It was a static theatrical scene, which was viewed through a little window. The "show" took place in a box. Often one end of the box, the opposite to that of the viewer, was lit up with a lighted candle, and between the peephole through which the viewer peeped and the candle, was a slide of isinglass, painted in bright colours. But not all peepshows displayed coloured slides, some had solid figures instead, like one eighteenth-century peepshow which showed Diana surprised by Actæon. The solid figures, cardboard cut outs, or painted isinglass scene usually depicted some fairly dramatic happening, like the scenes from the Battle of Waterloo, that Lord George Sanger's father used to carry about. Children's peepshows were much simpler. The owner of a peepshow would allow her friends a peep, on condition that they paid a pin, hence the expression: "a pin to see the peepshow".

Like the panorama, which is a glorified form of the peepshow, the peepshow proper is meant to be *peeped* at, not gazed at. Hence it is a good toy to make for parties, when it can be passed round.

No toy is easier to make. Get an oblong box, remove the lid, and punch a peephole in the centre of one end of the box, using an Xacto punch to do this. The peephole should be about half an inch wide. Now cut away the whole of the other end. Cut a sheet of stiff acrylic, an inch wider on the left and right sides than the end of the box. Mark on this acrylic sheet the size of the box end, and then score two lines down gently with a scriber to mark the lines where the acrylic overlaps the box. Later these two tabs will be folded inwards and glued inside the box with PVA adhesive. Cut out a Nativity scene, and colour it carefully with good quality water colour paint. Gold leaf can be added to the haloes of the figures by brushing on a little size and then laying down some gold leaf and rubbing it down. Never use tinsel for a project of this sort — leave this for the children to do. Once the figures have been painted, lay them aside.

Now get some transparent paint, such as diluted Humbrol enamel, and paint a fiery sunrise or sunset on the back of the acrylic sheet. Bars of alternate orange and red, brushed on horizontally across the sky, should do very well for this. If you like you can cut out the lines of the sunset from red and orange coloured transeal, and stick it to the acrylic.

The background scene of the box is now complete and you can turn to the main auditorium of the theatre. Cut out some trees and animals, paint them, and paste them on to thin card. Now fold over the tabs. Cut pieces of waste card of the same size and shape as the tabs and put them on the floor of the box, where the animals and trees will stand. Cut another piece of waste card, big enough to cover the whole of the end wall where the peephole is. These waste card pieces are put in to protect the cardboard from the spray coating that is about to be added, and enable it to take adhesive subsequently. Do not glue them in, just lay them on with perhaps a piece of Bostik to make them stick down.

Now spray the whole of the interior of the peepshow box with "frost" aerosol, or cover it with paste and scatter granulated polystyrene on top of the paste. Add artificial snow to the top of the trees, and make icicles by squeezing out plastic cement and letting it drip down in runlets from the branches.

When all these decorations have dried, remove the pieces of waste card. You now have patches of bare cardboard in the sides and bottom of the box which will take adhesive and to which you can glue first a square of mirror paper, with a hole cut to correspond with the peephole, at the inside end of the box, and then the trees and animals which are glued down by means of their tabs. The mirror paper will reflect the red glare from the painted acrylic sunset on to the figures. Paint the lid of the box a deep blue to represent the night sky and cut some small stars out of mirror paper, sticking them down irregularly here and there on the inside of the lid. Brush the inside rim of the lid with PVA adhesive and stick it down to the box. Finally glue in the acrylic end piece. Now cover the box, apart from the acrylic "window" at the end, and the peephole, with fancy paper.

When completed this peepshow is held against a fairly strong light to be looked through. It ought to be so effective that you can ask for *two* pins to see the peepshow.

Pepper's Ghost was one of the greatest scientific amusements of the nineteenth century, yet it is very simple to recreate in paper. It was not the ghost of John Henry Pepper, the Professor and Demonstrator at The Polytechnic, in London, that stalked the stage, but an illusion that he had devised. This illusion was staged at that peoples' palace of amusement, that occupied the place of the present college in Regent St., London. In those days the Polytechnic, the only one of its kind in England, was not a place of education at all, but rather what the Americans would call a "dime museum". For a trifling fee, the public could see the biggest electric eel in captivity, called a "torpedo". If they were prepared to pay a little extra, they could get an electric shock from the eel. If the eel happened to be off colour, they could always watch Pepper's Optical Amusements. These included magic lantern shows given on a magic lantern that was so big that the lenses had to be made from two glass sections, one concave and one convex, and filled with water.

The greatest success amongst the Optical Amusements was undoubtedly the ghost. In the middle of a play, a disembodied ghost would appear among the live actors on the stage and flit eerily about, apparently walking through the solid bodies of the rest of the cast. Nobody could guess, at first, how the trick was worked, until Pepper published an account of his device. This was how it was done.

Two stages were constructed, one above the other. The one below was invisible to the audience. Both stages were closed in with a sheet of plate glass placed at an angle of 45° to the stage, the top one partly, the bottom one completely. On the top stage stood the actors in ordinary dress. On the bottom stage stood the ghost, dressed in white and lit up by a powerful lime-light projector. The image of the ghost was reflected on the bottom sheet of glass, and cast by it on to the top sheet. As the ghost actor, illuminated by the powerful lamp below, moved about on the under stage, the ghost image was projected on to the upper stage, and appeared to flit mysteriously right through the other personages in the play.

This piece of theatrical "business" can be reproduced much more easily as a toy. Cut out a piece of Bristol board to the dimensions that Fig. 33 illustrates. Score the lines marked in the diagram lightly with a craft knife on one side of the card only. Bend the card over along the edge of a table, then make a trial assembly of the five parts of the box. Now punch a hole through the end wall of the box for the peephole. As before, use an Xacto punch (a $\frac{1}{4}$ in. one) to get a good clean hole. Next cut a sheet of acrylic to the dimensions given in Fig. 34 and score the lines marked half an inch in from the ends, so that the tabs can be folded over. This acrylic sheet is intended to produce the same effect as the sheets of glass on the two stages in the Polytechnic.

The whole of the interior of the peepshow is now sprayed with black poster colour to improve its reflective properties. The whole of the outside of the box is now covered with broken stone doll's house paper so as to make it look like the outside of an Egyptian tomb. The outside end with the peephole in it and the further inside wall (the one seen through the peephole) are also decorated so as to suggest an Egyptian tomb. From grey art paper a flat arch and two Egyptian pillars are cut and stuck down on the inside, while on the outside end a false door is also cut from grey art paper and stuck on. The peephole itself is framed in an "Eye of Horus" motif. A sarcophagus is positioned inside against the end wall.

When the tomb is looking suitably creepy and authentic, turn your attention to the Mummy's ghost that is going to haunt it. The ghost is cut from cardboard such as backing board, with the hands placed beside the body. Cut a recess for a square of MPT in the back one centimetre square. Round off the edges of the mummy, which is cut out with a piercing saw, with a round needle file. Cut some strips of white tissue paper a few millimetres thick, to suggest mummy bandages and swathe them round the mummy. Have a few hanging loose. Now paint the whole of the front of the mummy ghost with white poster colour,

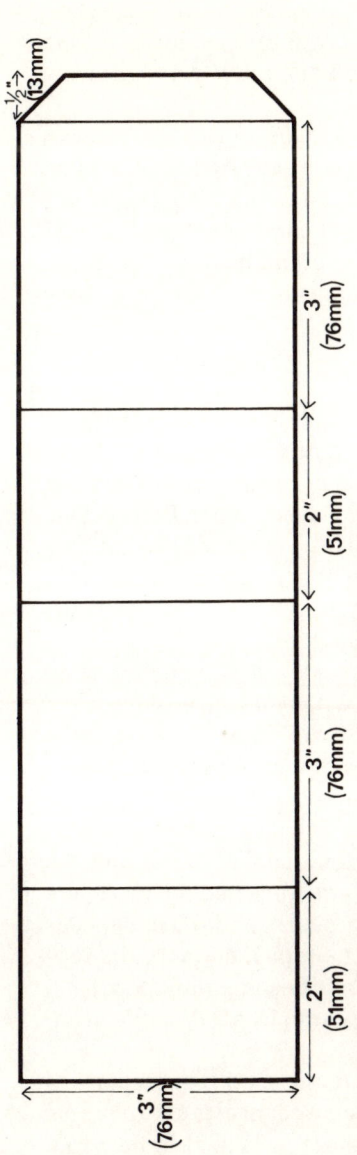

Figure 33. Dimensions of Bristol board for Pepper's Ghost Theatre box.

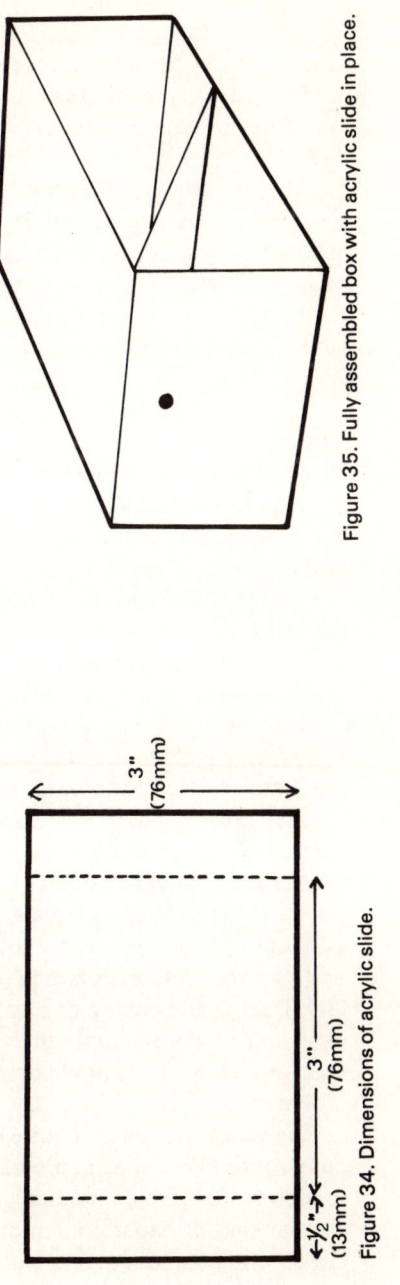

(Measurements along length: 2" (51mm), 3" (76mm), 2" (51mm), 3" (76mm); width 3" (76mm); corner 1/2" (13mm))

Figure 34. Dimensions of acrylic slide.

(3" (76mm) × 3" (76mm), with 1/2" (13mm) marked)

Figure 35. Fully assembled box with acrylic slide in place.

to which a little green has been added, giving a second coat. The ghost is now complete, except for a square of MPT which is cemented into the recess in the back with PVA adhesive, if need be after the bandages covering the back have been cut away first.

Now assemble the Pepper's Ghost Illusion Box, gluing with PVA to achieve a good join. The ghost is activated by picking up a small magnet, or a square of MPT, and attracting the ghost's magnet. The ghost lies on its back on the bottom of the box near to the peephole. It can be slid about so that its reflection glides about round its sarcophagus and appears to hover in a really ghostly way.

The Panorama

In some ways the Panorama is a sort of glorified peepshow. In other respects it is very much a toy in its own right. The panorama makes use of the artistic device of *perspective* to suggest space receding from the peephole or viewing point. Perspective, the concept that distant objects must be rendered so that they appear smaller, and finally the whole horizon disappears at what is called "the vanishing point" is an artistic device which many children, and some adults, find puzzling.

It is therefore well worthwhile making a panorama just to introduce a child to the idea of perspective. Because of its use of perspective, the panorama has always been a much more sophisticated toy than the peepshow. It was almost always professionally made, and like the peepshow, it is a toy that gives all it has to the viewer in a quick glance. The idea of the toy is supposed to have been suggested by the opening of the Thames Tunnel in 1829. This marvel of the age attracted many visitors and its sixty-four bays were full of toy sellers and souvenir peddlars. The bays, receding one behind the other, certainly did suggest one of the panoramas that soon became very popular – such as a view of Westminster Abbey with Queen Victoria being crowned.

The simplest method of making a home-made panorama is to construct a piece of what professional paper artists call *tôle*. This French word – which means just "sheet" – is applied here to a special kind of paper construction in which identical prints are cut up and positioned, one behind another, to create an illusion of depth. The prints are cut out with scissors and usually mounted on sheets of perspex in planes which recede one behind another. They are then mounted in a picture frame. Seen from the front of the frame, *tôle* looks not like cut-out sheets positioned one behind another a short distance apart, but like a three-dimensional sculpture — or a real life scene viewed through a window.

Looking round for a short cut to help me make a panorama, I decided that I would modify this technique. I despaired of ever obtaining identical prints, but consoled myself by deciding that I could easily photostat one print several times. I chose as my master print a picture from a child's book published many years ago. It showed the centre of Dublin as it was before "the Troubles". I decided that I would photostat this illustration four times and cut each out separately, mounted on cardboard, later positioning them in a box so that when they were viewed from the front, the different sections would be separated by spaces of a few inches, to give an illusion of depth and perspective. There would be cut out figures in the foreground just to carry on the illusion a bit further. The whole scene would be viewed from the nearest wall of the box. This would be covered with doll's house wallpaper with windows cut in it. The two windows on either side would be curtained, as though the curtains had just been opened in the morning. The middle window would, however, be left open and through the panes of glass (thin perspex divided by card window framing) you could catch a view of Dublin, with everyone hurrying off to work or school. It is much more dramatic to get a side-long peep at a panorama in this way than to be able to see the whole of it all the time. Some kind of peephole — like my drawing room window — also prevents the roof of the box in which the panorama is set up from showing.

I decided that I might want to make not one but several panoramas. So that I could use the same box to set them up in, I constructed one which would enable me to change the panorama scenery in a moment. It was cut from thin hardboard (Masonite), stuck together with Evo-stik. Small lengths of slotted plastic strip were stuck down the side, of the kind that can be bought in any model shop for making plastic models. Slotted wooden strip would have done just as well. The box had a removable top made of perspex which I had "frosted" by rubbing it with steel wool, to

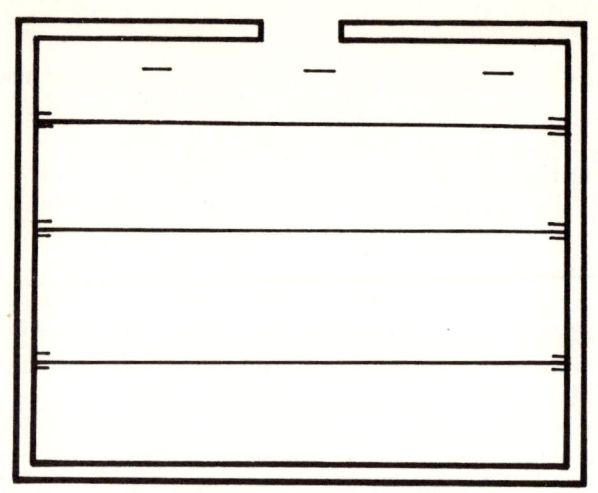

Figure 36. View of panorama from above.

let in light. The front was not stuck to the rest of the box. Instead it was removable and was screwed to wooden battens stuck to the floor and sides. This was done in order that it could be changed for another front when I wanted a different panorama.

I now pasted my photostated illustrations on to pieces of medium thick card. From one of these card sheets I sawed off the skyline above Trinity College, using a piercing saw. I slotted this into the first pair of slots back from the backdrop – this was a plain oblong of card which just fitted the back and which was sprayed a light blue with poster colour. Now I turned to the middle-ground scenery. The Bank of Ireland appeared in this, and as I wanted to have the bank right in the foreground I painted out the part where it appeared closest to the viewer with a mixture of Chinese white and Indian ink, so that it merged into the rest of the print as a blur. Then I cut off the top of the left hand part of the bank, and continued along the natural line of the roofscape. I also disposed of any figures that I did not want to appear in this plane of scenery.

I now turned my attention to what was going to be the foreground piece of scenery. I sawed down the left hand pillar of the bank, and along the line of the heads of people in the street, including part of the road in shadow, and also included the Rolls Royce on the right. Now, again with mixed Chinese white and

Paper Entertainments

Indian ink, I painted out a school girl and newspaper seller who were to appear as standing figures right in front of the window. Now I slid this third from the backdrop piece of scenery into its two slots.

All that was left to do was to cut out the schoolgirl and the newspaper seller from their piece of board. I left a tab below each of them so that they could be positioned in a wooden base (like the ones used for military modelling) and stuck down with Studio gum near the window. Using Studio gum meant that they could be removed without too much difficulty later.

As I was building up the panorama I screwed the front of the box on from time to time and glanced through the window, just to see how the whole scene looked from the point from which it would be viewed. If anything had looked out of place then I would have moved the slots backward or forward. The panorama was now finished except for a few minor touches such as sticking down minute squares of mirror paper on to the window panes of Trinity College and the street lamps. This made them look as though they were reflecting the sun.

All sorts of changes can be rung with panoramas. As I have already mentioned many panoramas that were made in the past were intended to be viewed by artificial light. There is no reason why a panorama should not be lit up from inside, perhaps with a timing device which slowly increases the volume of light, then dims it till it dies away completely. The scenery and figures in this panorama were static, but there is no reason why some of the figures should not be worked by strings, like those in the panorama box which Lord George Sanger carried about with him.

All sorts of basic ideas for panoramas spring to mind. It is not difficult to imagine a panorama of Venice, peopled by gondoliers in gliding gondolas, or one of a forest scene where herds of deer appear among the trees. A panorama of Arctic exploration with moving icebergs and snow that falls from a box in the lid of the panorama would also have a good effect. Panoramas need not be just for fun, they can be highly educational classroom projects as well. The idea of taking a peep appeals to all of us, young or old. Perhaps it goes back to the days when mankind had to keep looking round the corner just to see if it were safe to go on. As the panorama is a kind of miniature theatre, its possibilities are no more limited than those of the theatre itself.

7. Toy Theatres

The toy theatre has been the nursery of so many men of genius that it is difficult to regard it just as a toy. William Blake, Sir Walter Scott, Charles Dickens, Robert Louis Stevenson, G. K. Chesterton, J. B. Priestley, Paul Valéry, Val and John Gielgud are just some of the great dramatists, actors and novelists whose budding powers were developed by this toy — and who knows how many great men and women of the future might not be inspired by it today? If the toy theatre is to have an inspirational effect on our own children, however, it will have to be completely revitalized, as at the present moment it has almost died out through over-elaboration. What I am proposing in this chapter, then, is a complete "revolution in the toy theatre". Just why this should be necessary will appear when I say a few words about its history.

The toy theatre is one of the most British of all paper toys. It originated as a theatrical souvenir, a fairing bought by children who had been taken to the theatre by their parents. Soon the publishing of the printed sheets which carried a picture of a model theatre proscenium, and actors and scenery for particular plays came to be associated with a certain Benjamin Pollock, of Hoxton, London. Pollock advertised his sheets of plays as: "A penny plain and twopence coloured". Most of his young customers preferred to buy the black and white sheets and colour them themselves. The plates from which Pollock struck his prints were often engraved in an extremely artistic fashion. It was a positive challenge to seize a paintbrush and begin colouring when you saw these beautifully engraved actors and actresses, all looking more handsome, more beautiful and more talented than they ever could in real life. The young theatregoers would

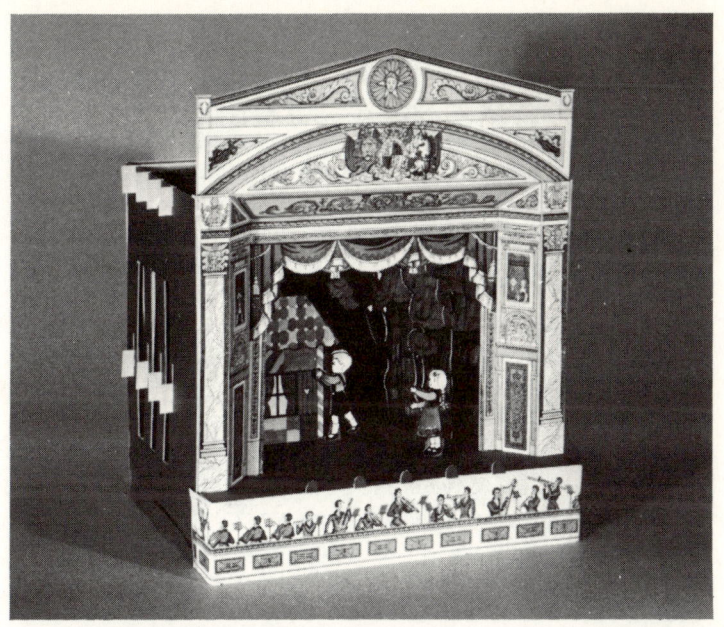

Figure 37. Toy theatre with Pollock proscenium and orchestra (*by courtesy of the Toy Museum, London*).

cut out the figures one by one, a long and difficult task, and colour them with water colour paints. They would then mount the feet of the actors on wire sliders, a sort of wire handle that enabled the character to be slipped in from the wings.

Altogether getting the cast, scenery and properties ready was such a task that little enthusiasm was left over to put on the play itself. Yet as the only important English dramatist who is *not* known to have played with a toy theatre remarked: "The play's the thing". Robert Louis Stevenson, a devotee of the toy theatre if there ever were one, recalls the feeling of disillusionment when all was ready and the show had to begin. "The purchase and the first half an hour at home, that was the summit. Henceforth the interest declined little by little. Two days after the purchase the honey had been sucked." Charles Dickens also recalls that the constructional methods employed to make up the characters did not always make for a good performance. He refers to the "besetting accidents and failures, particularly an unreasonable disposition in the respectable Kalmar" (a character) "to become faint in the legs and double-up, at exciting points of the drama."

I know, from my own experience, the labour involved in cutting out and colouring a Pollock play. Twenty years ago you could still buy sheets struck from the original plates (now they are collector's pieces well beyond the reach of the ordinary purchaser, and if you could buy a sheet you would want to frame it, not cut it up) I bought, cut out, coloured and mounted as *tôle* a play called *The Brigand*. I found that the characters, with their beautifully slim ankles, took a great deal of care in cutting out. The theatre which I built and which had a wooden stage and proscenium covered with a modern picture of an old theatre front, and which had in addition flies and battens, was too substantial for actors who weighed about as much as a postage stamp, and who could never fall through the wooden "boards" I made for them. It was large and there was nowhere to put it between performances. When lifted on to the table it scratched the top. The family tripped over it and everyone heaved a sigh of relief when it was consigned to the garage.

There and then I decided that if I opened a toy theatre again it would be on an entirely different model. I resolved to design a theatre which would resemble the present-day stage. It was all very well for Benjamin Pollock to sell theatres which showed a full orchestra, an elaborate curtain and proscenium, stage boxes with ladies in ostrich feathers and so forth, because in *his* day the lights in the theatre never went down, even during the performance. What was more, how could you put on a modern play in a theatre whose front was decorated with people in Regency costume?

I decided that I would design a theatre which looked contemporary. The proscenium would be functional and non-distracting. The whole theatre would fold away, so that it could be stored flat on a bookshelf, assembled in a moment, and if desired, be packed in an artist's portfolio, with the scenery and characters, so that it could be taken to a party. Nothing would be left about to get dirty or broken, and the actors would not, like the "respectable Kalmar" get faint at the knees, but glide in and out gracefully. The theatre itself would be so simple that it could be cut out in an afternoon while it would not take more than a few evenings to mount the characters and scenery. Redesigned in this way, I felt that the toy theatre might be ensured of a few

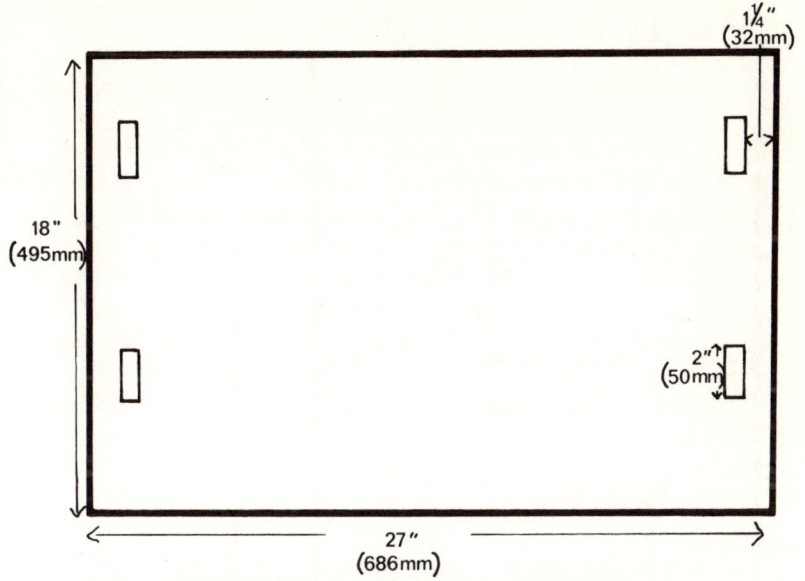

Figure 38. Dimensions of back wall of model theatre.

centuries more of life.

Begin work by constructing your model theatre out of hardboard. It is a box, three of whose sides hinge together. Stout hinges of book cloth fasten them together. The book cloth is pasted on to the hardboard with PVA adhesive and rubbed well in with a bone folder. The proscenium is the front of the box and in this sheet of hardboard there is the opening of the stage. The sides of the box have hooks cut in their ends and these hooks fit into slots cut in the third or back wall of the box. This fourth or back wall is cut wider than the proscenium front so as to allow for an overlap and room to cut the slots. The three hinged sides are bent into three sides of a square and the ends of the two side walls hook into the back wall so that the whole structure stands rigidly for performing purposes. The cutting out is done with a piercing saw or fretsaw. All the angles of the walls are verified with a set square before being laid out. Particular care is taken in cutting the slots and the hooks.

Besides actually holding up the theatre, each wall has a different function. The back wall carries a backdrop, a removable piece of scenery, pasted on to a thin sheet of board which can be

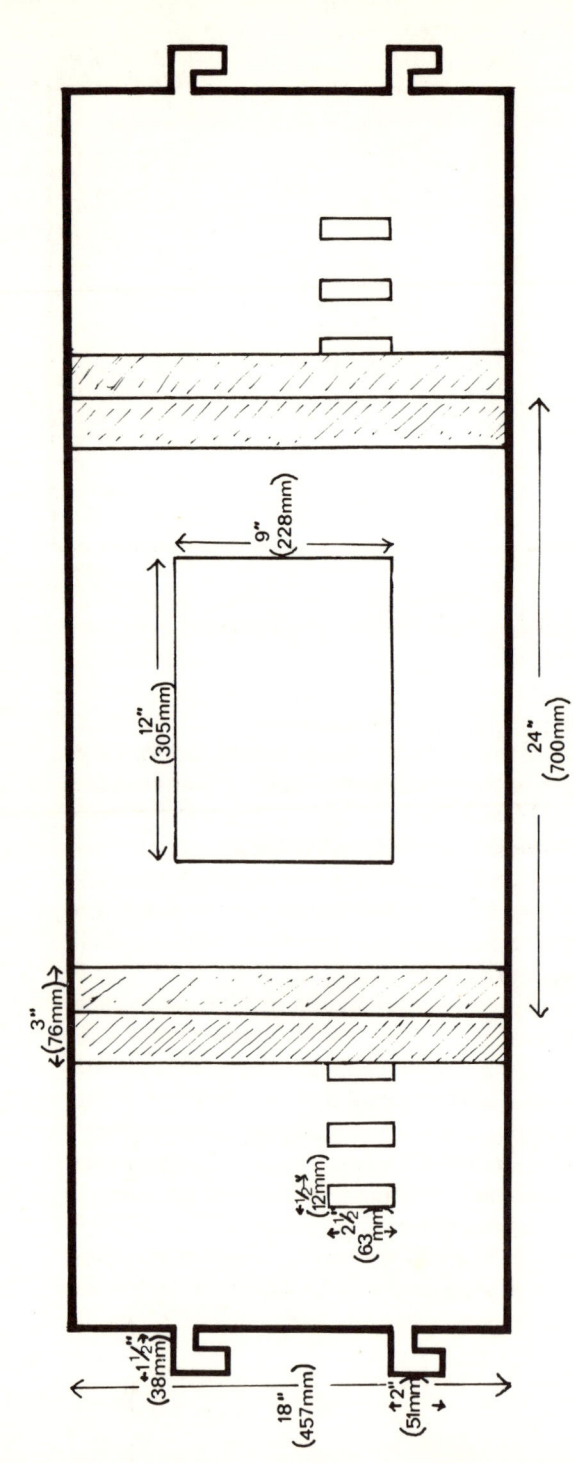

Figure 39. Model theatre with side pieces fixed to proscenium front by means of cloth hinges.

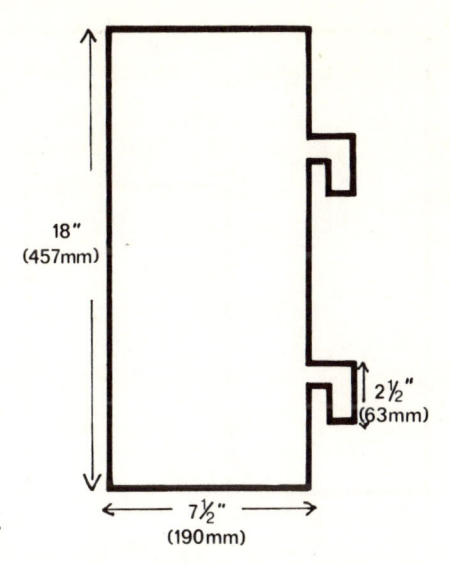

Figure 40. Model theatre wing.

18" (457mm)
2½" (63mm)
7½" (190mm)

simply clipped to the back wall with paper clips. This temporary fastening enables the backdrop to be removed in an instant.

The side walls are also slotted to enable wing pieces to be slotted into them. These wing pieces are connected by a bridge at the top to prevent them wobbling while in place. From time to time a transformation scene may be required in a play. This is a scene painted on an acrylic sheet which is semi-transparent. Once it is in place it ought to be removable rapidly so that it can create a dramatic effect by revealing the scene that lies behind it. Instead of slotting into the side walls, this transformation scene simply hangs from the top of them by means of a cardboard bridge with a thumb tag attached to it to make lifting easier. Besides carrying a painted scene, the transformation scene sheet can show scenery which is photostated from an illustration, cut out with embroidery scissors and pasted on to the acrylic with PVA adhesive.

The scenery and backdrops are illustrations photostated from old books, and simply pasted on to the backdrop or the wings with cold water paste. It is not difficult to find an illustration to use as a master print. Books on architecture are particularly useful for this purpose. The characters are also figures which have been photostated from an old book illustration – preferably from a Victorian book, which was almost always illustrated

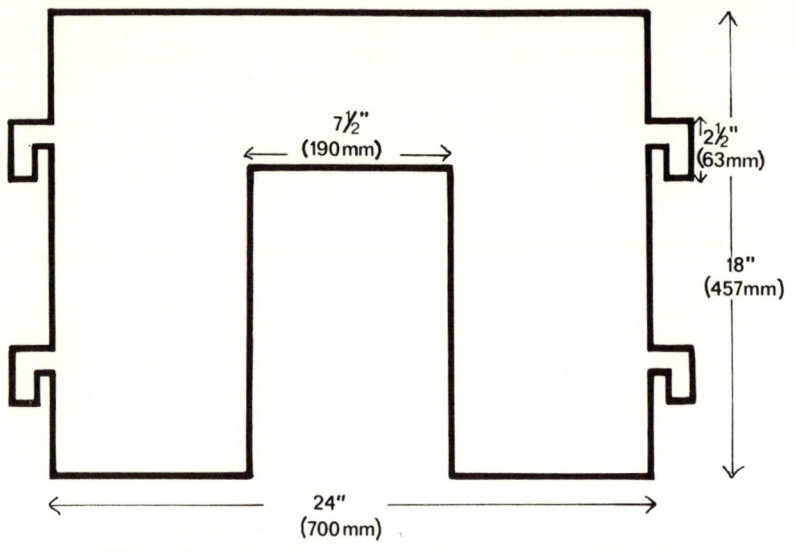

Figure 41. Scenery wings for model theatre joined by bridge at top.

with woodcuts, which reproduce well.

These characters are first cut from the sheet with embroidery scissors. Next they are pasted to the acrylic slider which will move them in and out. This slider, shaped like a blunt dagger, has a cardboard handle. It moves in and out of the lower slits cut in the two side pieces of the box. The acrylic slide moves right through to the other side of the box and passes into the slot on the other side, enabling it to be left at rest when not required to move about the stage. A typewritten adhesive label carries the name of the play and the character, and is stuck to the cardboard handle for easy reference. These sliders are stored, ready for use in a cardboard box such as an old shoe box, which is the same length as the slider. Slots are cut in the end of the box. It stands upright near the performers and the characters are placed in it in order of their appearance. Each slider handle, and the slot it slips into, is numbered with Letraset. The shoebox itself is given rigidity by having the top pasted on to the box rim. The box is labelled with the name of the play. You may have to make up a separate box for large sized characters, such as actors who appear on stage on horseback. As this kind of slider holder will not travel

Toy Theatres

very well, if you have to transport the stage to a party, make up a backing board album with a pair of sheets of stout paper pasted to each leaf just at the rim. In the sheets slots are cut so that the characters can be slipped into them. Bookbinding cloth makes the hinge for this album and the covers are tied together with tape.

In order to put on a play, the stage is placed on a table so that the bottom of the proscenium opening will be at the height of the audience's eyes. This position does away with the need to have "boards" on the theatre. The audience can see the feet of the actors, but not under their feet. Properties are moved in and kept in place by the same means as is used to move the actors. Keep properties to a minimum, because you need the slots in the side of your stage for your characters.

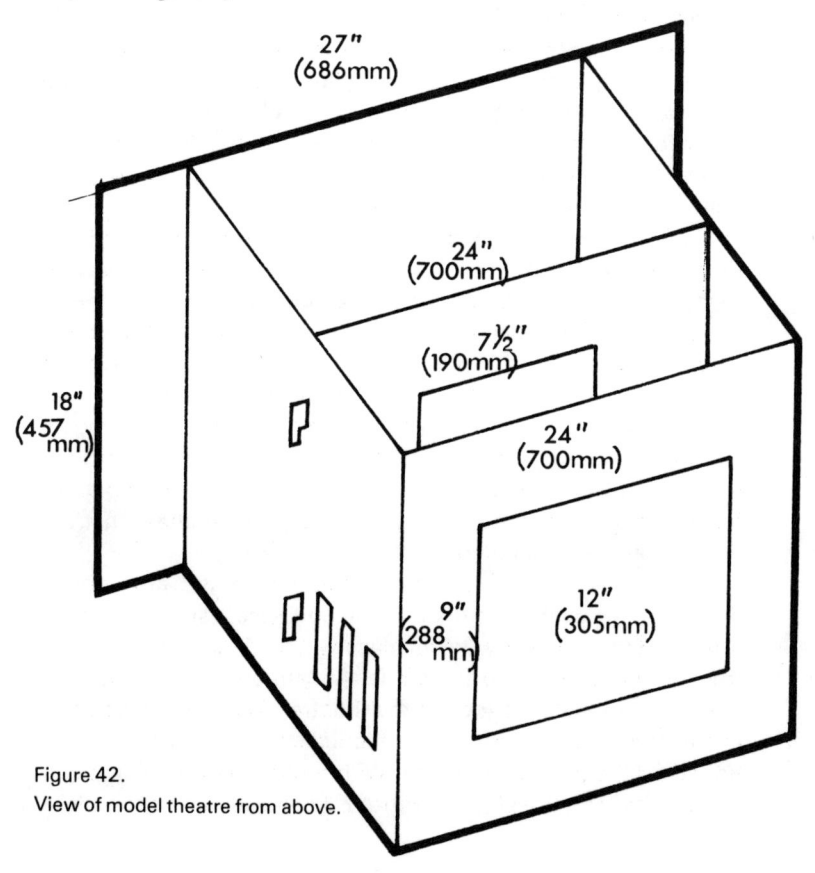

Figure 42.
View of model theatre from above.

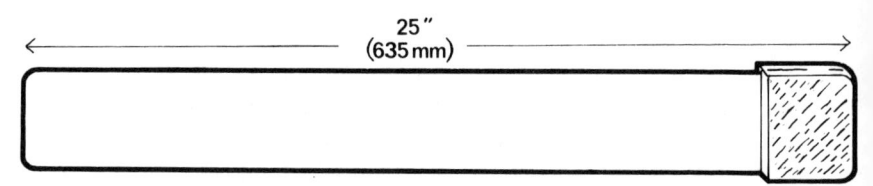

Figure 43. Acrylic slider for mounting model theatre "actor".

Light the stage by means of a small spot lamp directed on to the stage, directed through the top of the theatre. Do not make the same mistake that I did, and spend so much time making miniature lights that I found I was becoming a model electrician rather than a model impresario!

As you can see, what I have suggested is a recipe for instant model theatre. I give dimensions on my drawings, but you could double them if need be if you have properties to manipulate that would naturally be large, such as ships or spacecraft. You will find these dimensions suit paper "actors" very well, and the slider for the actor will not be too heavy to handle easily. The scenery and characters need not even be coloured. They will look quite effective in black and white, while if you want colour you could flood the scene with it from a differently coloured bulb. Even the task of cutting out such features of scenery as you want to include on a transformation scene, and the characters themselves, will come much more easily to you than it did to young Louis Stevenson and Charles Dickens. They did not have the benefit of really sharp tools, such as embroidery scissors, craft knives and stencil cutters. Do not forget to do all your cutting on a cutting board of backing board so that you do not blunt your tools. When you have to cut out a character, begin cutting at his feet and cut round him from right to left. Reverse these instructions if you are left handed.

As I have said already, the decoration of the proscenium should not be such as to distract the audience, especially as the room in which the show takes place will be darkened except for the light directed on to the stage. A plain but neat finish does however, enhance the look of the theatre. You might decorate it in one of the flower papers I mentioned earlier in this book. Why not cover the proscenium front with pressed flower pink paper and call it: "The Rosebud Theatre"? Japanese handmade block

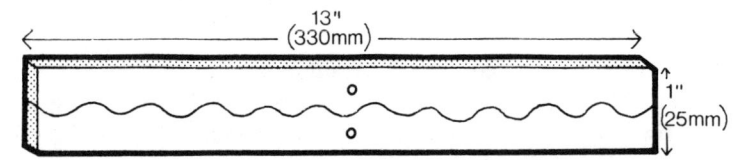

Figure 44. Cardboard batten to hold theatre curtain. Note the holes for attaching thread.

printed papers also make an attractive finish. If you want to add anything else, let it be very restrained, such as a paper cut out in white paper of a tragic and a comic mask.

Though not all modern theatres own curtains any more I feel a curtain is essential to the magic of the stage. You can make a drop curtain that can be lowered and raised very simply, on the lines of the transformation scene which I described a moment ago. A cardboard bridge carries the curtain, which hangs suspended from the top of the sides of the theatre "box". The curtain is made from sheets of paper rolled into waves to resemble a fabric curtain hanging in folds. The cardboard bridge which supports the curtain has been sawn into a wavy line with a piercing saw. The two halves have been pulled apart and the paper curtain glued between them with PVA adhesive. The curtain has been rolled into billows by rubbing it in one direction and then in the other with the edge of a ruler. You can make any sheet of paper curl towards you or away from you depending on which way you press the ruler edge. The rolling billows have been made permanent by spraying them with artist's fixative so that the folds of the curtain are permanently in place. Finally, the bottom of the curtain has been finished off with one of those trimmings you can buy in paper shops, or haberdashery counters, a strip of gold fringe. If for some reason you cannot find a gold fringe, then make one for yourself by getting a strip of good quality art paper half an inch wide and the length of the curtain. Draw a line down the centre of this strip and below it cut tassels with a craft knife, using a straight edge. These tassels should be about a quarter of an inch wide. Now paint the whole strip, tassels and all, with gold poster paint. I always use "Plaka" gold poster paint and find that this gives a good, deep colour but there are plenty of other good proprietary gold paints such as "Goldfinger".

As soon as the paint has dried out, the strip is stuck on to the bottom of the curtain with PVA adhesive, so that the tassels reach just to the bottom of the proscenium opening. This drop curtain is dropped in and pulled up by means of a cardboard thumb tag on the bridge.

Toy theatre plays should be full of action. They should aim at the effects which are impossible in the real theatre. When a building is blown up, for instance, its roof can really fly up into the air. Everything should be done to make the actors look as live as possible. The slider that holds them can be tilted slightly backwards and forwards, altering the play of the light on their faces. They can even be made to appear to start violently by just flicking the handle of the slider with a finger to make it vibrate.

The whole of the drama is open to the toy theatre, but as all small play groups face the same difficulty, shortages of copies of the play, why not start with a strong scene from Shakespeare, such as the ghost scene in *Hamlet*, or the one in *King John* where Hubert prepares to murder Arthur? It should not be too difficult to collect enough volumes of Shakespeare for your needs.

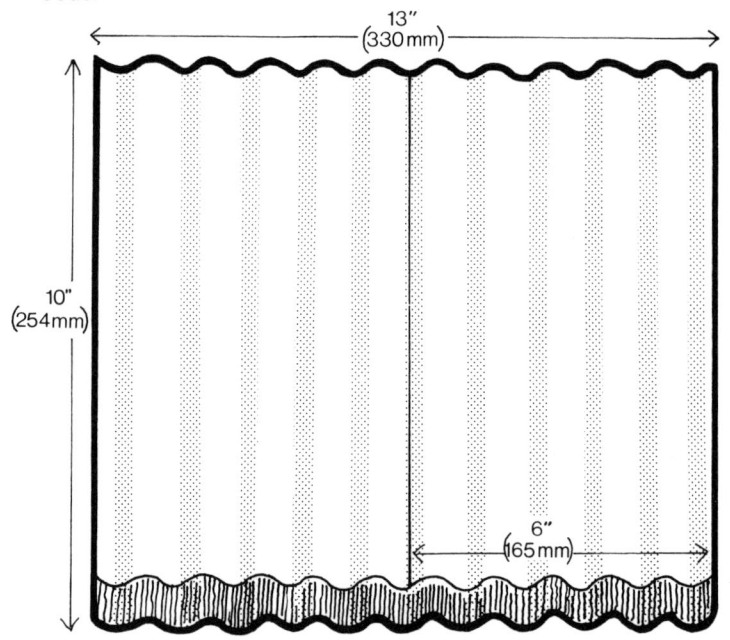

Figure 45. Rolled paper curtain with gold fringe for model theatre.

The Shadow Theatre

The shadow theatre is another wonderful old form of the juvenile drama which is now being done to death by unnecessary over-elaboration. Nowadays writers on puppet theatres treat the shadow theatre as an art form which can only flourish to the accompaniment of plentiful electric light and an elaborate stage setting. Just the contrary is the case. The classic shadow theatre, that of Java, Bali, and China, was at its zenith before electric light was known about. The gentle light of a candle cast a magic on to the simple fabric screen which, so observers tell us, has largely dissipated now that the old style puppets are displayed in the harsh light of an electric bulb. So to get the best out of shadow theatre, decide here and now to make do with candles, even if you have to create your own candles, with several wicks, to get the right light.[1] Do not construct an elaborate stage. Instead, simply find a large second-hand antique picture frame without the picture or glass, and frame inside it a sheet of tracing paper or perhaps two sheets pasted together. Frame this in the old picture frame by cutting backing board strips which line its interior recesses and then tacking in the tracing paper with a few drawing pins. Prop this frame up on a table draped with some old sheets with a pair of wire legs twisted through ring screws screwed into the sides of the frame half way up. Position the candle, which for safety's sake is floating in a bowl of water[1] about two feet behind the screen. What could be simpler?

Now put the energy that you would otherwise have wasted on making an elaborate shadow theatre into the puppets themselves. In the Far East these puppets were made from transparent buffalo parchment. Cinemoid is a good substitute. If you cannot get cinemoid, use acrylic and paint it. The shadow figures need only have one movable piece, the arm. A separate rod of split cane runs from your hands to the foot of the puppet, and another to the arm. We will assume that you are kneeling on the floor with the candle burning in its bowl of water propped up on some kind of stand on a level with the table. The screen is on the near side of the draped table, and you are in between so that you can easily press the puppets, with their bamboo rods against the tracing paper. The puppets not in use are stuck in holes cut in a

---

[1] See the author's *Candle Making*, Teach Yourself Books, Hodder.

shoebox that has been treated in the same way as the one required to hold the sliders for the toy theatre.

The characters for the shadow play should look magical rather than practical. Scenery and stage properties can also be introduced on the end of a split cane rod. One of the beauties of using a candle for the shadow play is that, as John Henry Pepper found out more than a hundred years ago, you can make your figures dance and perform the most weird antics without moving them at all. All you have to do is to move the candle.

8. Hot Air Balloons and Spinners

The Hot Air Balloon
Though the papers are full nowadays of news about hot air balloonists, little has been done to revive the sport of model hot air ballooning, so popular with Victorian boys. Paradoxically, it is much easier to make a hot air balloon from paper now than it was in Victoria's day.

Victorian schoolboys used two main methods in their approach to the balloon. The first was to mass-produce them by cutting out balloon gussets from doubled sheets of paper. The gusset, so cut from tissue paper, was composed of an isosceles triangle on top of two squares set end on end with another triangle at the bottom. Rough block cut gussets of this sort ensured that the balloon could be made very quickly and this was an advantage because the balloons were expendable, being intended to burn out during the flight. Balloons were often intended to carry up fireworks, so they were usually sent up at night. Hence their builders were not too worried about what they looked like.

An "instant" balloon of this sort can be made from tissue paper of two colours, say white and red. Tissue paper is sold in sizes that vary more than for any other kind of paper. One standard size in which it can be bought is 20 by 28 in. (50 × 75 cm). From this standard size, make a balloon according to the following pattern. Draw out a template from thin card of four 7 inch squares set one on another, making an oblong 7 in. by 28 in. The top and bottom squares of the template are cut down into tapering points as shown on the diagram (Fig. 46).

Lay this template on a double thickness of tissue paper consisting of one white sheet laid on a red one. Cut round the template with a sharp craft knife, cutting two gussets at a time. Now

|← 7" →|
(178mm)

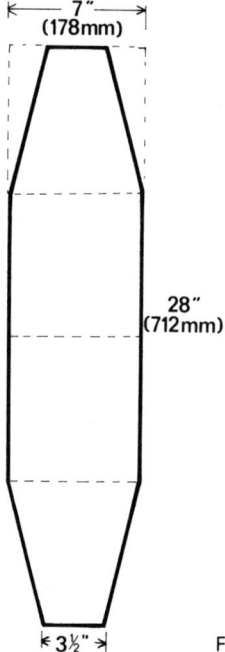

28"
(712mm)

|← 3½" →|
(89mm)

Figure 46. Template for balloon gussets — made from a card divided into four 7 in. squares.

go on till you have cut eight gussets. Once they are cut, look at the gussets to examine whether or not they have become crushed during the cutting-out process. If they have lay them in a pile and iron the pile with a medium hot iron. Now make up some cold water paste, and using a paste brush, paste the edges of two gussets at a time. Bring the edges together and rub down the join with a bone folder. Do not forget to paste a red gusset to a white gusset. Put two pairs of joined gussets together to make half a balloon. Now paste the two halves together. You should be left with a balloon which has a rather ragged finish but is roughly spherical. Tidy it up by finishing off the top of the balloon by cutting a circular crown piece. Cut a large washer in the shape of a disc 6 in. (152 mm) wide with a hole punched in the middle with an Xacto punch. Get a length of strong thread (nylon does very well) 8 in. (200 mm) long. Tie a loop in it and knot it. Push the loop through the hole. Spread out the threads on what will be the underside of the washer and paste them down with PVA adhesive. Allow the threads to dry, then paste the washer to what will

Hot Air Balloons and Spinners

be your crown piece. It is a circle a foot in diameter. Rub it down well. The loop should hang freely. The crown piece is intended to strengthen the top of the balloon and to help prevent hot air escaping. The loop is for carrying the balloon, or for hanging it up if it is stored, and the washer is intended to keep the loop in place.

Now strengthen the bottom vent. The width of the bottom vent will vary with the size of the balloon. The bottom vent (the hole at the bottom of the balloon) should not be too wide, or else too much hot air will escape. It must not be too narrow either, or it might come in contact with the burner of the balloon and catch fire. Cut a strip of tissue paper to the pattern I illustrate, the length of the diameter of the bottom vent of the balloon. You can work out what the length is by measuring it with a piece of string. In the middle of the strip paste down a length of thin nylon string, then paste the whole of one side of the strip and attach it in place outside the bottom vent. Tuck the flaps inside the orifice of the balloon, and stick them down, making sure that the nylon thread goes right to the bottom of the vent. The thread is intended to strengthen the fabric and also to enable the burner to be hooked on below it with four hooks.

Before fitting the burner, make the balloon as airtight as possible by spraying it with artist's fixative. Most fixatives nowadays are made from synthetic cellulose solutions, but those marketed some years ago were made from shellac, which gives off poisonous fumes when burned. Make sure which kind you are using. Copal varnish is a good substitute for fixative; it is perfectly safe to burn. Apply the varnish to the balloon in spray form if possible, as this will make a better seal. Hang the balloon up by a thread attached to its loop and inflate it with cold air from a hair dryer before spraying. Re-inflate it from time to time to ensure that it retains its spherical shape. When the varnish is dry, apply a second coat.

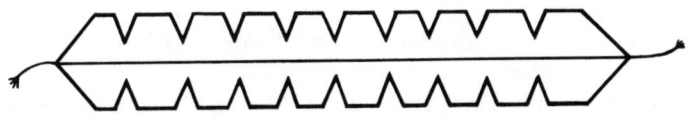

Figure 47. Shape of tissue paper to go round bottom vent of balloon.

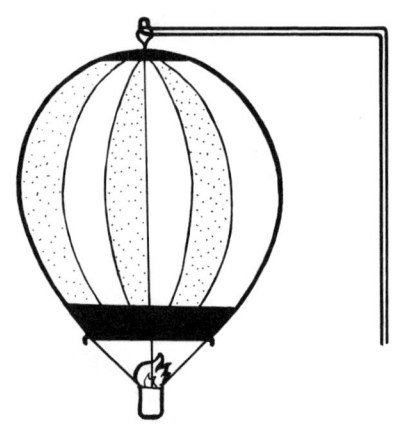

Figure 48. Finished balloon, showing carrying handle of wire, burner attached, gores and strengtheners at top and bottom.

Now make up a burner from a metal capsule with four wires with hooked ends which are cemented to the capsule with Araldite or some other epoxy resin cement. The wires are attached at right angles to one another to spread out on all four sides of the capsule. Very fine wire, such as thin garden wire, or bellwire, will do ideally for these wires. They must be sharpened very slightly at the free end with a file. The hooks at the ends of the wires are hooked into the nylon thread girdle and bent over so that they support the burner.

The balloon is now ready for lift off. A hot air ascension is a serious business *which should never be carried out without adult supervision*. It is indeed preferable that the balloon *should be launched by an adult*. A balloon 2 feet in diameter needs 4 cubic feet of hot air to fill it, so it will take some time to warm up.

Get someone to hold the balloon up in the air, preferably on the end of a hooked wire. Then fill it with hot air by holding a blow torch operated by a Butane gas cylinder underneath, but not so near that it sets fire to the fabric of the balloon.

When the balloon is full of hot air, put a tablet of solid fuel into the burner. Release the loop from the hook. Hold the loop with one hand and light the tablet with the other. Once the tablet is well alight the balloon should lift off. Do not put too much fuel into the burner for this or any other subsequent flight or the balloon may fly so high that you cannot retrieve it. Always make flights in an open space where the balloon will do the least possible damage if it lands with the burner still alight. This is some-

Hot Air Balloons and Spinners

thing that it ought not to do but it is always the unexpected that happens, as my service in the R.A.F. taught me.

A short time ago I mentioned that there were two main styles of constructing balloons in the Victorian schoolroom. Now it is time to discuss the smartly tailored ones, which were cut to a tapering gore, exactly the shape of an orange which had been peeled by cutting equally spaced slices from top to bottom. Some text books even give mathematical formulae for designing balloon gores (or gussets, the word means the same). There is no need to go to these lengths. A rough guide is that a balloon 3 ft. in diameter needs 12 gores, each 18 in. in length (half the circumference of the balloon), and three inches in width at the equator. Each gore tapers towards the ends.

The Spinner

All sorts of wind and convection current paper toys can be made. I have not even mentioned the common windmill, but I have illustrated an adaptation of it invented by myself, called a spinner. As you can see from the illustration, this toy is made very simply by gluing to a painted card shape the old refill tube of a biro pen, which has been cut to size, then washed out with a pipe-cleaner

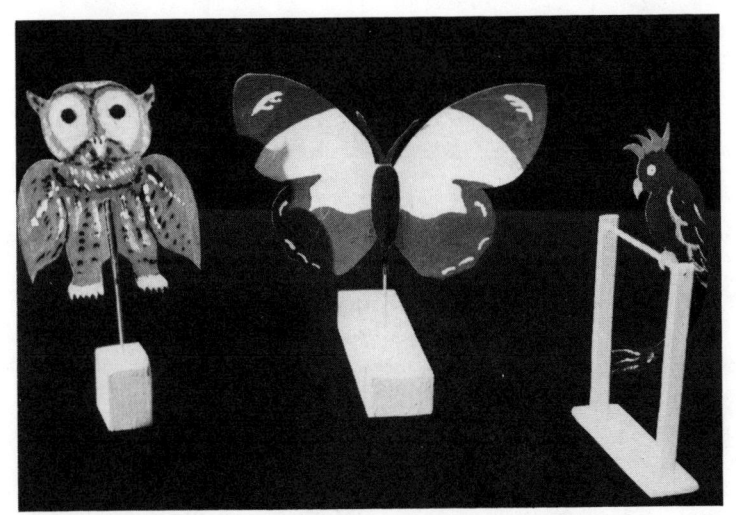

Figure 49. Two spinners and a rocker (*by courtesy of Hodder & Stoughton*).

and methylated spirits. The tube rests in a spike of thin bamboo, glued into a wooden stand. The spinner revolves splendidly given a stiff breeze. To make it revolve when sitting on top of a heat source, such as a radiator, just stick card fins, angled like the two different blades of a propellor to the sides of a spinner. The rising air currents will then turn it round and round.

9. Miscellaneous Toys

The Jigsaw Puzzle
No toy or game can be too simple so long as it is a success. The jigsaw undoubtedly is a success. Jigsaws have been in continuous production since the eighteenth century, when the first jigsaws appeared. They were then very much of an aristocratic toy for the favoured few as they were cut from fashionable and expensive mahogany, but even at that date they were a distinctively paper toy as they could not have been made but for the paper picture stuck to the front. Even nowadays, when plastic has replaced paper in so many toys, jigsaws still have a paper facing. Between the eighteenth century and our own day there intervened the Fretwork Era, when thousands of enthusiasts sawed out jigsaws from plywood using hand or treadle operated fretsaws. Then at about the start of our own times, plywood was abandoned for good, and cardboard became the basis of all jigsaws. Hobbyists felt unable to cope with the new material and gave up jigsaws altogether.

Nonetheless, nothing is easier than making a jigsaw from paper and cardboard, provided that you know how to set about it. The tool for jigsaw making is a piercing saw. Properly used, this will cut such a fine and such a clean line that the jigsaws you make yourself will be indistinguishable from those cut by machine tools in the factory. By following the few, easy steps I outline you will not merely be able to make all the jigsaws you want for a tithe of the cost of buying just one, but you will be able to choose your own subjects. Jigsaws are not merely fascinating toys, they can be extremely educative as well. It was with this value in mind that I chose the subject for the jigsaw illustrated here. So many tourists have stopped me and asked for information about the old City Churches in London, without my being able to give a very coherent answer as to where they were, that I decided to learn something about them. I bought a reproduction of an old print from the Victoria and Albert Museum bookshop for just a few pence. It was entitled: "Enlarged detail from the Panoramic View of London from Westminster to the Tower, 1749, engraved by S. and N. Buck." It shows all the old churches.

I could have obtained the raw material for quite a number of jigsaws for nothing at all. Posters and illustrated leaflets, which are printed on good paper and are therefore highly suitable for jigsaws, can often be got for the asking. The tourist information kiosk outside St. Paul's Cathedral gave me several decorative posters which were out of date. At the British Tourist Authority, 64 St. James St., London, S.W.1, I picked up, amongst other material, a leaflet advertising Montacute House with a beautifully reproduced portrait of Queen Elizabeth I. It was just the kind of material I needed to make the small size of jigsaw that is ideal for stocking fillers or birthday presents.

Having obtained the picture for the jigsaw puzzle, the next step is to acquire some backing board. This is, as has already been noticed, a thick cardboard which is very like the kind of board on which commercial jigsaw puzzles are mounted. Start by measuring the picture you are going to use, then mark out the area that it covers on the backing board. Allow one eighth of an inch all round as the paper will spread by about that measurement when damped and pasted. Now cut off the square or oblong of backing board that is to take the jigsaw from the sheet of backing board. Use a straight edge and a sharp craft knife for the job. Damp the underside of the jigsaw puzzle print with a sponge and a little cold water. Lay it on a sheet of waste paper, face downwards and paste the underside of the print with cold water paste. Start at the middle and work outwards. Now fold over one pasted end of the sheet and stick it to another pasted end. Paste the oblong of backing board and lay the print on top, paste side down. Rub it gently on to the backing board. A soft duster or Jiffy cloth and a bone folder are particularly useful for this task. Be particularly careful not to trap any crumbs of paste between print and board. Do not allow any bubbles of air or paste to stand out as unsightly blisters.

Figure 50. Drawing lines for a jigsaw puzzle, using the special jigsaw ruler.

When you are satisfied that the surface of the print can stand inspection, lay it on a flat surface, cover it with a sheet of waxed paper, and lay a board, such as a piece of hardboard, on top. Place a heavy weight on top of the hardboard. When the print has dried to the board, repeat the whole process, but this time paste the back of the mounting board with a sheet of waste paper, about the same thickness and quality as that of the print. This back layer of the "sandwich" is of course to prevent the "drag" of the print "drawing" the board out of true and warping it towards it.

When the "sandwich" has dried out completely mark out the lines of the puzzle where it is going to be sawn into bits. There should not be too few pieces, otherwise the puzzle will be too easy to assemble, nor too many otherwise it will be difficult both to put together and to saw out. A glance at the lines of a commercial jigsaw puzzle will act as a useful guide here, and for the actual mechanics of drawing the lines, try the device which I illustrate in Fig. 50. It is a jigsaw ruler, cut from stout plastic, with interlockings at irregular intervals. With this ruler, lines that are roughly parallel are drawn across the surface of the jigsaw, either horizontally or vertically. The position in which the ruler is placed is varied somewhat to prevent the siting of the pieces becoming too predictable. Once the main parallel lines have been laid down, they can be subdivided by drawing freehand lines between them, not forgetting of course to draw an interlock on each side of every jigsaw piece.

There are several different types of interlocks and by changing the kind you use, it is easy to add variety to your jigsaws. To illustrate what I mean, I have reproduced a geometrically interlocking design from a nineteenth-century Japanese pattern book. Apparently the Japanese made jigsaw puzzles at quite an early date and the toy may even have originated with them.

The line with which you mark out the division of the pieces should be clear, but fine. A Rapidograph pen line does very well for this purpose. Before you start cutting give the whole surface of the puzzle a coat of matt acrylic varnish. This coating will lengthen its life and help to prevent it becoming grubby. Now lay down a newspaper on the floor of your workroom to help you collect the pieces as they are cut. Nothing produces more frustration than a missing piece! Set up a sawing pin, a plank with a

Figure 51. A geometrical pattern used in Japanese jigsaws of the nineteenth century.

Miscellaneous Toys

"vee" cut in the end clamped to your bench with a G clamp and lay the jigsaw puzzle board on the plank so that your cut will come in the vee. Do not alter your position to cut out the various pieces, instead swing round the jigsaw so that you are always cutting in the same direction. Saw with a regular, up and down motion, avoiding a slanting cut. Try to imagine that you have a power jigsaw and that you can only saw in the absolutely vertical direction. If you find that you are getting tired, put the jigsaw aside and finish it later. The essence of a good jigsaw is a meticulously cut division between the pieces.

When you have collected all the pieces, calculate what size of box will be required to hold them, make up a box according to the pattern I give, cutting it out from thin card with a craft knife. Once pasted together with PVA your box will be a good deal stronger than most commercially made boxes. Cover it with fancy paper and stick to the lid a typed label with the jigsaw puzzle title.

The Pantin

The Pantin is another simple toy, simple but effective. It was so effective that when Pantins first became the rage, back in the days of Louis XVI, the police banned the toy, on the grounds that pregnant mothers would become so accustomed to seeing it everywhere that they would produce children with distorted limbs. The French pantins were modelled on court shepherds and shepherdesses, Harlequins and Columbines, not the best of models perhaps, because there is always an element of caricature about this toy, and shepherdesses and Columbines are too dignified for the rôle. Harlequin is all right of course, you can easily imagine him doing the splits. Once the pantin had crossed the Channel, and become acclimatized in England under the name of "jumping jack," it was for many years made up as a caricature of the French monarch, Napoleon III. I have given one or two illustrations of pantin patterns on traditional lines.

You can make this toy from quite thin card, such as Bristol board, but as you are, I hope, making it to last for as long as possible, it is best to use backing board. Start with one of the simpler designs which I give, such as the German pantin (which was the same model that was popular in America, where, no doubt, it was introduced by German immigrants). Trace or copy the

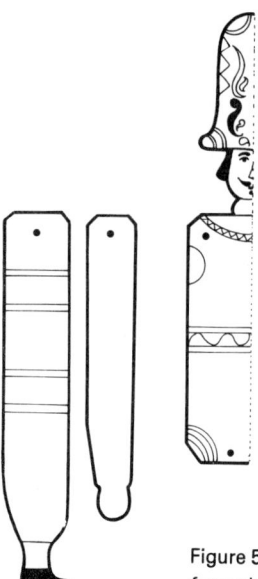

Figure 52. Leg, arm and half design of body for early American pantin.

design of the body and head, legs and arms, on to backing board. You may decide to enlarge all the designs I give considerably. The larger the pantin is the more fun it will produce. Using an ordinary twist drill, drill holes for the legs and arms at the spots where they are attached to the body. Before painting, put the toy together and slip split rivets into the holes to hold legs and arms to the body. Try the toy out to see if everything swings freely, and if it does not, reposition the hole.

Now paint all the pieces with artist's size. This can be bought in small pots and has to be heated up in a saucepan of water. Set the parts aside to dry, and then when they are thoroughly dried out, paint them all with a ground coat of white poster paint. Now add the top colours which should be bright, also in poster paint. Put in the details of the face with black poster paint, using a fine brush.

Now give the jumping jack its permanent assembly. Take some of the split rivets which I mentioned a moment ago, which can be bought from any hardware store, and push them through the holes you have drilled in the body, arms and legs. Traditionally the arms and legs were rivetted in place *behind* the body, but you may find that you can get more action out of the

Miscellaneous Toys

toy by placing them before it. Once the split rivets are in place, force the clefts of the rivets open gently with the blade of a screwdriver. Flatten out the points and tap them flat with a plastic covered hammer. If you want to, you can put a thin washer between the opened rivet and the back of the leg and arm.

Now string the jumping jack, using nylon thread. Tie a thread about six inches long to the top of the head and attach to it a plastic or wooden ring of the kind that you can buy in toyshops such as John Galt's. Tie a short length of thread to connect the holes in the tops of the arms and legs of the figure when they are in the *down* position. Knot another and longer thread, in the exact middle of this shorter one. Do this for both arms and legs, not forgetting to attach the plastic rings to the ends of the strings which you can get your fingers through. It is better to have separate leg and arm threads on this first model, so that both legs and arms can be worked independently. To activate the pantin, just dangle the figure by its head string and pull the other two.

My second pantin figure, Napoleon, is slightly more elaborate

Figure 53. A Napoleon III pantin.

to make, but easier to operate, in that one ring works all the moving pieces of the figure. The thread to which the ring is attached passes through a hole in the back of the figure which supports the flapping coat tails.

Make up the figure as before, riveting arms, legs and moustachios. Cut out the cardboard bridge, cut a vee in it for the string to pass through, slip the moustachios and arm thread attachments to it, then tie the leg attachment to it below the bridge. The coat tails should be cut from shiny green bookbinding cloth and stuck to the bridge with the shiny side of the cloth showing.

Painting instructions for the figure are as follows: coat, shiny green (the Napoleonic colour) with gold buttons. The buttons can be punched from gold foil paper with an Xacto punch or by one of the punchers used for perforating paper for clip files. They should be stuck down with PVA adhesive. Breeches and waistcoat are white, boots and hat black, cocade red, white and blue, with the red on the inside.

The Thaumatrope
The Thaumatrope is another toy that has been undeservedly forgotten. It is the simplest of all paper toys to make. From the moment, in 1825, when Dr. John Ayrton Paris, President of the Royal College of Physicians, invented the thaumatrope, till today hundreds of thousands must have been made, but nowadays there is not a single one to be seen anywhere. As the label of a box of thaumatropes sold in 1826 put it, "The Thaumatropical Amusement [serves] to Illustrate the Paradox of Seeing an Object which is out of sight, and to demonstrate the faculty of the Retina of the Eye to retain the impression of an object after its disappearance."

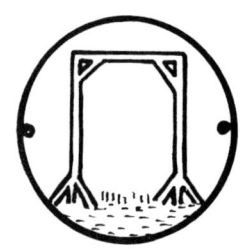

Figure 54. The original thaumotrope invented by John Ayrton Paris.

Miscellaneous Toys

The inventor of the toy, Paris, had hit on the idea as a demonstration of "the continuity of vision" to his students. He made up a cardboard disc, with a gibbet on one side and a man hanging from a rope on the other. A string was attached to either side of the disc. When the strings were held tight and the disc twirled, preferably by being blown smartly at its top, the toy whirled round and round, and the eye was presented not with the separate spectacles of a malefactor *and* a gibbet, but of one hanging from the other. As John Ayrton Paris no doubt discovered for himself, the important factor to remember when constructing this toy was that the hanging man had to be placed *upside down* in relation to the gibbet. Why did Dr. Paris choose such a gruesome subject? Possibly because the Anatomy Act had just been passed and most medical subjects were still condemned malefactors.

Other subjects of a more cheerful kind used for thaumatropes at the time included a bald headed man who put on his wig when the disc was twirled, a rider who bestrode his horse, a rat or bird in a cage, and a cat catching a mouse. The whole idea of the cinema probably started with this, the first of the continuity of vision toys.

To make a thaumatrope draw a circle with a compass on Bristol board. The circle should be two inches in diameter. With a scriber make two holes one eighth of an inch from the sides of the disc; fit two lengths of thread to these holes and tie them securely. Now draw a suitable picture on one side of the disc, and its complementary picture on the other side. Hold up to eye level and blow.

The Rotater

The rotater is one of the many toys that have been suggested by some practical object. When I was at school we were encouraged to match colours by means of a device made from two discs of cardboard which were superimposed on top of one another and joined in the centre with a rivet. There were windows cut in the top disc which showed through to what was written on the bottom one. Supposing you wanted to find a contrast to the colour red, you simply turned the disc till red appeared in one of the windows. In the window on the other side of the disc you would see green.

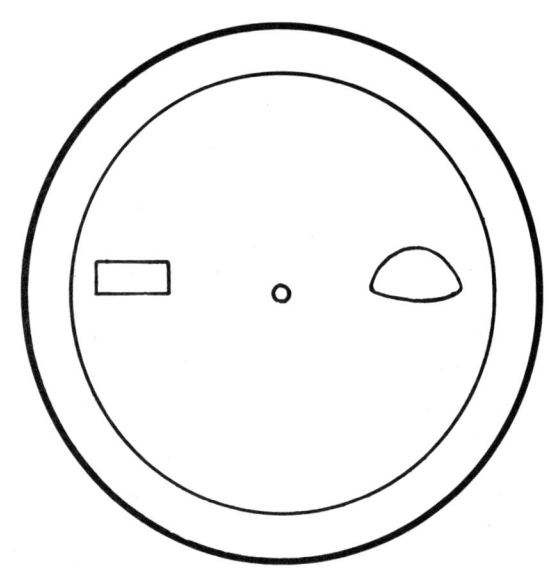

Figure 55. Rotater toy.

As a toy which requires some manipulation and one that has educational potential, the rotater has great possibilities. Try making one which combines an animal recognition chart and spelling toy.

Cut out two discs from backing board, marking them out with a compass. Both are eighteen inches in diameter. There are two "windows" on the top disc, one on either side of the centre rivet. One, an irregularly shaped opening, is going to show the animals that have to be identified. The other, a square opening, contains the animal's name. The top disc is painted green with poster colour. It can have trees collaged on to it here and there, with a few railed enclosures to suggest a zoo.

Cut out the discs with a piercing saw. Drill a hole through the exact centre of each. Paint both discs, sizing them first. Paint the underside disc white. Now cut out some pictures of animals from old magazines, using the irregularly shaped "window" as a frame to make sure that they are the right size. Temporarily offer up the top disc on to the lower one, holding it in place with a split rivet. Move the top disc round over the lower one, finding as many positions as you can and marking them in both windows with a pencil. Now separate the discs once more and stick down

Miscellaneous Toys

the animals in the irregularly shaped openings. Type out some self adhesive labels with the correct names of the animals and stick them in. Leave one space without an animal's picture. Instead stick down in the irregularly shaped opening a piece of mirror paper which will quite fill it and make up as a label: "Giant Donkey". When both discs are completed cover them with Transeal or varnish them with artist's water colour varnish.

The Paper Barometer

Paper toys that are very easily made but which produce a good deal of interest amongst children are weather toys. A paper barometer can be made up on the lines of the Victorian paper instrument which I have illustrated from John Henry Pepper's book. The cowl of the monk is hinged on to his robe by a rivet such as a brass paperclip. A piece of catgut attaches the cowl to the robe. When the weather is dry the catgut contracts, when it

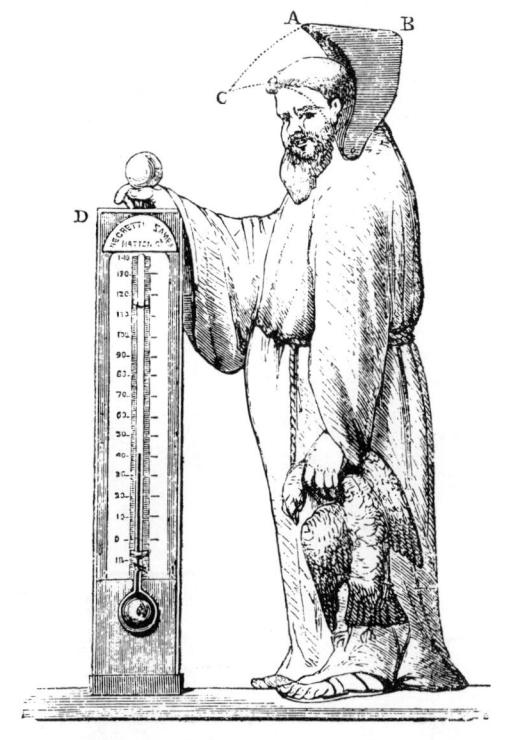

Figure 56. A paper barometer, operating by means of the catgut affixed to the cowl.

is damp, and likely to rain, the catgut expands. Make sure that you are really buying catgut when you buy the string to make this toy. The "D" string of a banjo or a guitar, which is the thickest string, is suitable for this purpose. Take care it is not a nylon string. The outside of the packet should tell you what material the string is made from.

The Weather House
If you want to you can easily make a weather house on the traditional model by constructing a cardboard building, with an opening at the front for a circular cardboard turntable. On this turntable are positioned a cardboard duck — for wet weather, and a peacock — for fine weather. The circular turntable hangs from the centre of the roof, which is made up of cardboard and which simply rests on top of the walls. The whole of the weatherhouse is finished in doll's house stone and slate paper.

The Paper Flower
Another "weather prophet" is the paper flower. Make up an anemone from the paper shapes which I illustrate (Fig. 57). The leaves are cut from green blotting paper, the centre and pistils

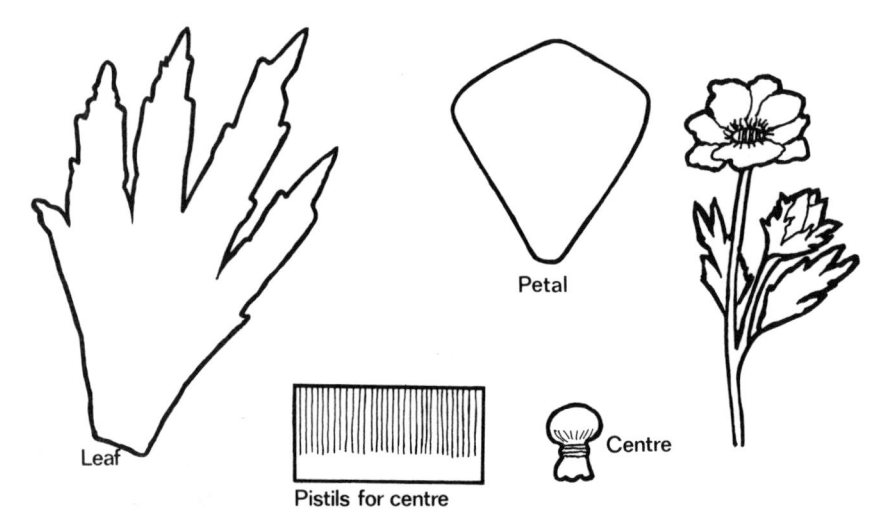

Figure 57. Parts of the paper anemone, with completed flower on right.

Miscellaneous Toys   137

from black crêpe paper, and the petals from pink blotting paper. Make up a complete flower in pink blotting paper, sticking the petals together with Copydex, or any other adhesive that will not dissolve in water. Now steep the completed flower (Fig. 57) in a strong salt solution until the whole flower is impregnated with salt. Finish the flower with the other paper pieces, which are not soaked in salt. When completed, the anemone will be pink in wet weather and white in dry weather.

Party Puzzles
All sorts of party tricks can be contrived from paper, almost at a moment's notice. They can be used to fill up the dull moments of a party, and they are also very useful for using up paper leftovers. These paper party toys should be made up in sets so that they can be handed round amongst the guests.

Make up some puzzles, such as the three geometrical ones I illustrate (Fig. 58), from thin card, surfaced with some decorative paper. Make up card squares with the two "lazy dogs" traced on to them. Invite the guests to turn them into "lively dogs" with

Figure 58. Geometrical puzzles with "shapes".

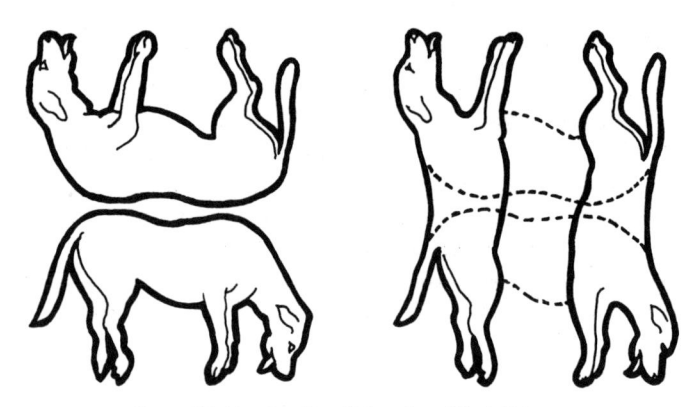

Figure 59. Turning "lazy" dogs into "lively" dogs.

two pencil lines (Fig. 59). Make up the dying serpent I illustrate (Fig. 60) from crêpe paper and roll up the sides and tail in the way I illustrate. Put a few drops of water on this toy and it will writhe about realistically. Cut a paper circle of paper such as I illustrate (Fig. 61), stick a small lead weight to the underside and position it on an inclined board so that it can defy gravity by rolling uphill. As a final party trick, offer to step through a playing card. Just cut the card in the way illustrated (Fig. 62), open it out and step through it.

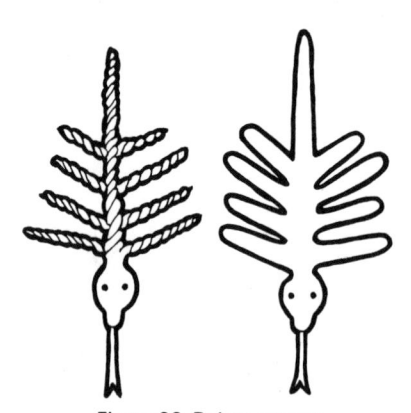

Figure 60. Dying serpent.

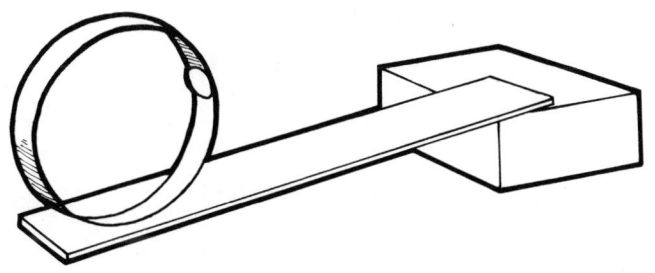

Figure 61. Rolling a paper hoop uphill.

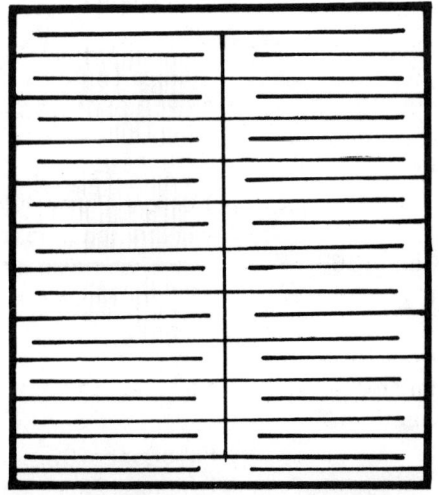

Figure 62. By cutting along these lines, you can step through a playing card!

Alphabetical Index of Toys

Air Battles, 36
Air Circus (wall game), 32
Airfield Buildings, 33–5

Chess, magnetic, 30
Chinese General, 28–9
Climbing Game, 38

Daruma, 44
Deep Diving Game, 36
Designoscope, 71
Diorama, 88
Distorting Mirrors, 82
Doll's Head (papier mâché), 43
Draughts, magnetic, 30

Glove Puppets, 44

Heliograph, 67
Hot Air Balloon, 119
   Filling with hot air, 122

Inu-hariko (Japanese toy), 47

Japanese Tumbler, 44
Jigsaw Puzzle, 125

Jumping Jack, 129

Kaleidoscope, 75

Magnetic Chess and Draughts, 30
Mexican Festival Toy, 43
Mexican Paper Doll, 20
Military Figurine, 57, 58, 60, 61 (see also 29)
Military Models from Masterprints, 51

Ninepins, 47

Panorama, 102
Pantins, 129
Paper Barometer, 135
Paper Dolls, 20–8
   Books for, 27–8
   Framed Pictures for, 27
   MPT Application for, 24
   Wardrobe for, 25

Paper flower, 136
Party Puzzles, 137

Index

Peepshow, 97
Pepper's Ghost, 97
Periscope, 79
Picture Frames, 27, 29, 117
Planes, Balloons and Helicopters for Air Circus, 33–5
Polyoptic Mirrors, 81
Praxinoscope, 83
Puppet's Head (papier mâché), 43

Rotater, 133

Shadow Theatre, 117
   Puppets for, 117
Spinner, 123

Thaumatrope, 132

Tibetan Chess Pieces, 30
Toy Soldiers, 49–62
   Battlefield Accessories, 62
   Cutting out Figures, 56
   Full-face Figures, 52
   Mounting Pieces, 53
   Profile Figures, 52
   Wargame from Ancient China, 63

Toy Theatre, 106–16
   Constructing, 109
   Curtain for, 115
   Lighting, 114
   Pollock plays, 106
   Scenery and Characters, 111

Weather House, 136